ELF ANTICS

The Definitive Parent Playbook for
5 Years of Mischief-Making

By Elf Delphine

COPYRIGHT

Cover design by: **nskvsky**

Book Interior Designer: **Farhan Shahid**

ISBN number: 979-8-9917622-0-5

Library of Congress Control Number: 2024921671

Printed in United States

Table of
CONTENTS

INTRODUCTION

Hi, I'm Mr. Delphine (that's del-FEEN, not deli-fine, thank you very much). I know, it's not the most exciting name, but I didn't choose it. The kid I'm assigned to did. If I had my way, I'd sport a name that screams strength, like *Schwartzenkoff*. Or perhaps a name that highlights my sensitive side, like *Alejandro*. But alas, elves don't get to pick their own names. Instead, some genius thought it would be a great idea to let a toddler—you know, those mini humans who are obsessed with anything "potty" related—make this decision. So, here we are - Mr. Delphine it is! I suppose it could have been worse. A colleague of mine was contracted to work for a family whose 3-year-old named him Mr. Tinkles.

Anyways, let's cut to the chase. I'm here to guide you with the unvarnished truth about this whole business of inviting a Christmas elf into your home to make your family's holiday season more "magical." With all those viral social media posts showcasing picture-perfect elf scenes around people's homes, you might think this gig is purely giggles and fun. But I'm here to let you in on a little secret: it's work. And I mean a LOT of work. And guess what? It's all unpaid! That's right; you'll be shelling out cash left and right for the *privilege* of pulling off these elaborate shenanigans. And your kids? Well, they may or may not show an appropriate level of appreciation, given the amount of time and effort that went into setting up each antic. It's right up every masochist's alley!

A bit too blunt? Ok. But it's the truth, and that's what this book is all about—the hard facts of hosting an elf and surviving the chaos that ensues.

Now, you've made a smart move by picking up this book. While it can't make up for your naivety in signing on to have an elf invade your home under the guise of spreading a little Christmas cheer - let's be real, that probably wasn't your brightest decision - at least you won't be left to your own devices. Because, let's face it, THAT would probably be a full-on disaster!

TIME FOR A REALITY CHECK

Let's talk about what you're getting yourself into here. You're committing to something that'll likely outlast most major appliances. Sure, in the beginning, it'll seem like it's all fun and games. But when your kids are tucked in bed, and you're practically passed out on the couch from sheer exhaustion, you'll suddenly realize that you have no clue what your elf will be doing tomorrow. And just like that, reality will hit—you've used up every fun and easy idea in your arsenal. At this point, panic will set in, and you'll frantically search the internet for any idea that will get you through one more day.

And thus starts the destructive cycle of just trying to make it one day at a time through the elf season. From this moment on, the Twelve Days of Christmas will bring on a level of stress known only to those brave souls who have been asked the dreaded question, "May I speak to you for a moment?".

If you're reading this and your kids haven't yet met the family elf, then:

ABORT MISSION! ABORT MISSION! ABORT MISSION!

Seriously, ditch the elf. Pretend you're Nancy Reagan and just say no. Listen, I'm just trying to help you actually enjoy the Christmas season without the hassles of planning, scheduling, and preparing. In other words, imagine what your life was like before having kids – remember that freedom...spontaneity...unfettered selfishness?!? Without an elf, all those can yours again... after your kids have been tucked away for the day. Go ahead, visit Margaritaville every night! Or relax in your recliner, spooning sugar cookie dough out of the tube while binge watching every Hallmark Christmas movie made since 1982. There's no late-night climbing on ladders or frantic last-minute decoupaging. Just relaxing evenings to yourself, with the freedom to be as self-absorbed as your little heart desires. And don't you think you deserve it?

When you have an elf, you can forget about flying off for those last-minute December holidays. The family I'm assigned to hasn't taken a pre-Christmas vacay since 2008. Whenever the topic comes up, the kid says, "But then we'd miss out on seeing what Mr. Delphine is up to! I don't want to go." And a pouty kid does not make for a fun vacation, so that's that.

Remember, Christmas cheer doesn't come cheap. It takes props to work our elfish magic. You might think you'll get your money's worth out of those props – you've convinced yourself that your kids will surely play with them for years to come, right? But let's be real—you KNOW they'll end up in your next Goodwill haul when you Marie Kondo your house looking for a "fresh start" for the New Year. That's money down the drain, all to put a fleeting smile on your kids' faces. If you're smart, you'll just take them to Chick-Fil-A, order a peppermint shake, and call it a season.

What? Am I coming across a little too strong? Think I'm overreacting? After all, how hard is it to come up with a couple of weeks' worth of antics?

I get it. But what about next year? And the year after that? And the year after *that*? After your first year's blazing success, are you just going to go cold turkey and quit, traumatizing your kids for the rest of their lives? Do you want them to think they're unlovable because their elf didn't return the next season but the elves of all their friends did? And seriously, do you think your kids will actually LOWER their expectations for what your family's elf will do when visiting your house next year? Hmm, I bet you didn't really think all that through, did you?!?

Face it: you're going to have to up your elf's game... every... single... year. Sure, in the beginning, your kids might be delighted just to see the little guy playing cute with all their toys. But that's going to grow old...and quickly. Most parents, after realizing this, start relying on the internet for a little elf inspiration. And once you start down that slippery slope, there's no going back.

It'll take hours just to find a few antics that are worthwhile. You'll have to scroll through blog after blog, entering your email address just to get access to what the blog promises to be the "most hilarious stunts ever," only to feel cheated when you find the ideas stink. Not only are you right back where you started from, but now you're going to be getting 50 emails a day from the blog owners urging you to check out the websites of their affiliates for "even more fun elf ideas." Pretty soon you're clocking in as much time searching for "funny elf scenes" as you are working your normal day job. Several hours will disappear at a time while you go down different rabbit holes, with little or nothing to show for it. And then you'll just end up repeating the whole process the next day. Face it, you're doomed.

To keep the kiddos impressed, your elf's antics will start to take on a life of their own – gradually getting more complex and messier. Trust me, you'll know by the look on their faces when you've let them down because you were too tired or lazy the night before to stage a truly epic or hilarious stunt.

Oh yeah let's talk about that. It's all about endurance, and it makes the U.S. Navy SEAL's Hell Week look like a spa retreat, because you won't have had a good night's rest since the Thanksgiving weekend... before your first child was born. You'll need to dig deep into whatever energy reserves you have left to stage these antics after your kids have gone to sleep, even on those days when you're ready to drag yourself to bed two hours before your kids have even had their dinner. In other words, it'll feel like you're in a never-ending marathon throughout the holiday season.

For those of you who have a partner and think that everything will be a breeze because you'll have two sets of hands—let's be honest here. Do you REALLY think your partner is invested in this elf-tastic venture as much as you are? You KNOW your expectations for the season's antics are much, much higher. Think about it—who bought this book? Exactly! So, lower your expectations back to the realm of reality and just plan to tackle this whole elf thing on your own.

Like I said earlier, this is at least a five-year commitment. And if you're in one of those households that keeps churning out kids every couple of years, you may be looking at a life sentence! So do the math and decide if your sanity can take the hit. Then, by all means, introduce the family elf to your kids.

Still feeling delusional? Ok, fine. Let's do this.

START WITH A GAMEPLAN

Over time, if you don't have a solid game plan, then elf season has the potential to turn into a major production and consume every waking moment of your life. You'll end up dreading the month of December like it's bathing suit or tax season.

That's exactly what happened with my family's mom. After a stellar debut my first year, she couldn't wait to repeat the fun. So she scheduled my next year's visits to start on December 1st. "What was she thinking?" you ask. Clearly, she wasn't! Talk about overdoing it—that's 24 days of pressure! After wasting my best elf antics in the first week because she was so excited about them, we were left with stale ideas for the rest of the season, which, by contract, I was still expected to pull off.

After that crash course in holiday stress, she learned the hard way that a game plan is an absolute MUST before my arrival. It led to many panic attacks, jolting her awake at night, her mind racing through potential scenarios. This annual anxiety fest kicked off every June, when she realized she had less than six months before the season's chaos began. She created computer planning files that even Franklin Covey would admire and spent all her free waking moments on the internet, trying to find something...ANYTHING...that would be a success without involving a bag of powdered sugar, 60 hours with a hot glue gun, or 36 family-sized bags of Skittles!

I share this as a not-so-gentle reminder that if you don't rein things in from the get-go, this whole elf season could spiral into a production worthy of a Mr. Beast video.

So, here's the gameplan:

STEP 1:
Wait For It...Wait for It...Go!

Do the math: the earlier your elf arrives each season, the fewer peaceful hours you'll have to enjoy it. So, let's stick with a 12 Days of Christmas theme that's slightly modified so that the twelfth day is on Christmas Eve. That means your elf should debut on December 13th and head back to the North Pole after the morning festivities on December 24th. This approach gives you enough days to pull off a variety of antics without sending you spiraling into a mental health crisis. But some people these days just seem to thrive in a climate of craziness and chaos, so if you identify with that sentiment, I've included more than 30 extra ideas for antics so you can get your groove on a little earlier in the season.

STEP 2:
Commit to a College Student's Bedtime

Don't even think about waiting until morning to set up each day's antics because (A) you'll spend the night sleeplessly worrying about getting everything positioned in time before your kids wake up, (B) your kids will wake up earlier than usual and catch you in the act, forcing you to come up with a convoluted lie that won't be believable because you haven't had a drop of coffee yet, or (C) you'll oversleep and be startled awake by panicked, crying children who'll think your elf has died because he hasn't moved since yesterday morning. None of these scenarios is good, so just embrace the challenge and stick to a late-night setup routine. The exception to this is if you only have teenagers since they operate on the same sleeping schedule as vampires.

STEP 3:
Take It Easy, Tiger

Slow and steady wins the race. Remember, it's not just about this year—look at the long-term picture. Space out hilarious or elaborate antics with simpler ones. Or, start with low-key stunts and build up to your grand finale. Be careful though. The closer you get to Christmas, the busier it gets. So, cut yourself some slack and schedule easier activities for those days when you know you'll feel rushed or worn out.

Each of the antics in this book can easily be replaced by another. If you're not up for one of the suggested activities, feel free to swap it out for something less elaborate. But try to stick with the same overall theme (e.g., hilarious, messy, easy to pull off, quiet but cute). That way, you won't find yourself stuck with similarly themed activities that are all leftovers by Year 3. But hey, who am I to tell you what to do?

STEP 4:
Shop Like it's 2020

Remember those COVID-hoarding days when people snatched every item in sight, turning garages into makeshift Costco warehouses? We're going for a similar effect, just scaled down a bit.

Pick up a large storage bin that's opaque. For those of you asking for a friend, opaque means you can't see through it. When you're out and about, and you spy something that may come in handy for a future elf antic, snag it. You may not use it this year, or even the next. But once you hit that five-year mark—or, if you're planning on going rogue and substituting your own plays for some of the ones in this book - that bin is going to come in handy.

Create a budget and stick to it. The idea is to use what you already have in the house for most antics. However, if you stumble upon unique items during your shopping sprees, let your creativity run wild! Aldi's, Michael's, CVS, Walgreens, Marshall's, TJ Maxx, HomeGoods, Hobby Lobby, and any dollar store are fantastic for finding unique, budget-friendly gems. Of course, there's always Amazon and Etsy to fill in the gaps. And don't forget about clearance holiday items the week after Christmas. Toss them in that bin for next year!

My family has already had the *Birds and the Bees* talk and the *That Nice Person Trying to Be Your Friend Online May Be a 62-Year-Old Pretending to Be an 11-Year-Old* talk. But they haven't had the *Who is Mr. Delphine...Really?* talk yet, and let's face it—kids know better than to ruin a good thing. When it comes to me, they've settled into a *Don't Ask, Don't Tell* policy.

Some items pictured in this book were bought three years before they made their debut! Many a festive day has been saved thanks to the contents of our bin. But just a heads-up: avoid hoarding food items for multiple years—common sense, right?

STEP 5:

Location, Location, Location!

Shake things up, folks! If you want to keep the magic alive, it's time to think outside the obvious spots. Think of this as an epic game of Hide N Seek, with me being the lucky one who always gets to hide.

Each day, let me spread my festive cheer across different rooms in the house. Mix it up! Save me a spot in the bathroom one morning and let me commune with the rubber duckies. The next day, I could be having a snowball fight with the stuffed animals on the dining room table. Trust me, your kids are going to love the thrill of finding out what your family's elf is up to, so make them work for it. You get to sit back and watch the madness unfold, and your elf gets to be the star of the show.

STEP 6:

Make Sure Your Elf Shows Some R-E-S-P-E-C-T for Your Child's Safety and Privacy

In our household, I follow two essential rules during my seasonal visits. First, my antics should pose no danger, particularly when the kid wakes up in the morning to see what I'm up to while his parents are still snoozing. We certainly don't want any of the little ones - or my animal friends – getting hurt. This is why I steer clear of any shenanigans outside, in the family car, or in the garage. We want to avoid any temptations for kids to wander off and explore unsupervised in potentially dangerous areas.

Second, it's crucial to respect kids' privacy and sense of security while they sleep. This means my kid's bedroom is off-limits for any of my antics. I also avoid his parent's bedroom, allowing them to catch a few extra winks of sleep in peace while their kid is joining up with me.

STEP 7:

Include Some Mischievous Messages

I like to think of myself as a bit of a jokester and leaving a note here or there adds a little fun to my antics. Sure, my notes are usually misspelled and scribbled with capital and lowercase letters mixed up, but what can you expect from an elf with the humor and education level of a 5-year-old? While typing them out on a computer is perfectly fine, I find that kids cherish the handwritten notes. I've included some of the wording I've used in my notes over the years for some of these antics.

STEP 8:

Remember – Don't Reinvent the Wheel

This book doesn't claim to have all new antics for your elf's adventures. In fact, the majority of these ideas can be found in other elves' playbooks all over the world. You've heard the expression "time is money," right? That's what this book is all about. Saving you countless hours of idea-gathering. Every antic that's included in this book was a hit in my family's home, and I think your kids will love them too. So, don't exhaust yourself trying to reinvent the wheel every year — go with what works! And spend that time you're saving doing something you love.

I'm sure booksellers would say this book belongs in the "Holidays and Celebrations" section. However, I personally classify it as a self-help book, as it'll save your sanity—and maybe even your marriage—since you won't be stuck spending hours scouring the internet for daily ideas. Make sure to fully read the antic you're planning to do ahead of time so you have an idea of how much time (and money) it will take to pull off. I'm sorry to say it, but my family could easily be featured on that show *Hoarders*. This has made my antics easy to pull off because they already had the stuff lying around somewhere in the house. Since they had 8 animated figures that had been collected over the years, I could easily pull off the Animatronic Band antic without having to purchase anything else. But would my family's mom have chosen that antic if the family didn't already have those figures? No. Because that would eat up all the money budgeted for coffee runs. And priorities are priorities. At least, that's what my family's mom says.

HOW THIS BOOK IS ORGANIZED

There are hundreds - if not thousands - of creative ideas floating around the internet that other elves have successfully pulled off. However, while some may look Instagram-worthy, many aren't worth the effort and expense, or simply weren't a hit with my family's kid. Trust me, after spending a decade with this family, I've had my share of flops when it comes to antics! That's the beauty of this book: I've only included the 93 antics that were a hit. Sure, I could probably share an equal amount that didn't make the cut, but I won't dare repeat them when it's time for my next elf assignment!

Although I do have a few antics that involve underwear and toilets, I steer clear of anything too gross. So, no chocolate poop or farts in a jar here! I also skip the risqué antics you might see from other elves. Mischievous? Absolutely! R-rated? Not my style. But no judgments here – if that's your family's way of spreading Christmas cheer, more power to you! My family prefers to keep things light, and, yes, admittedly a bit corny, even as the kid has grown older.

Within the following pages, you'll find a 5-year game plan. It assumes your kid will be about 4 to 6 years old for their first elf season. If you're starting earlier than that, the plan will still work as written. However, if your kid is older than 6, you may want to substitute some of the Year 1 and Year 2 antics, which are tailored for younger audiences. That's why I've included an additional 30+ activities – plenty of alternatives to ensure you find something that will be a hit with your little one!

The antics are ordered day by day, so your child won't really know what to expect next. One day's antic might be cute and heart-warming, with the next day's hijinks quite hilarious. Feel free to reorder the activities over the 12-day period to fit your schedule and energy levels.

5 YEAR ELF ANTICS PLAN

YEAR	DAY 1	DAY 2	DAY 3	DAY 4	DAY 5	DAY 6
1	Arrival 1 Introducing... Me!	Bubble Bath	All Aboard the Shoe Shoe Train	Story Time for Toys	The Perfect Hiding Spot	Despicable Bananas
2	Arrival 2 Floating By Dropping In	Snowman	Whirligig	Finder's Keepers	BrownEEz	Naughty! Naughty!
3	Arrival 3 Billboard	Floor is Lava	Orange You Glad It's Morning?	Charmin Snowflakes	Breakfast to Go	Singing for Santa
4	Arrival 4 Can You Tell Who's Back?	Flying Gumballs	Washing Day	Make Room for Candy!	Potty Songs	Snowball Catapult Fight
5	Arrival 5 Balloon Cascade	O'Chipmus Tree	Homework Helper	Taste Tester	PicELFso	Coat Closet Rave

YEAR	DAY 7	DAY 8	DAY 9	DAY 10	DAY 11	DAY 12
1	Indoor Snowman	Sippy Straw	TP Patrol	Vitamins Help Candy Canes Grow	Just Throw Your Kid's Underwear on the Tree	Breakfast is Served!
2	Worst Christmas Cookies Ever!	Shoe Shine	Bakery Shop	Magic Milk	Stockings Filled With... Underwear	Scavenger Hunt #1 Seek & Find
3	Scavenger Hunt #2 Riddle Me This	Ironing Out a Few Wrinkles	Frisbee Fun	Popcorn Palooza	TP'd Tree	You'll Never Guess What This Gift Is!
4	I'm a Little Tied Up Right Now	Chicken Wing, Chicken Wing	Silly String Battle	Reindeer Lessons	Toilet Bowl Toothbrush	Game Night
5	Sticky Wipe	Vertical Blinds	Retribution	Roasted Elf	Bowling for Root Beer	The Bowl of Champions

I've also created a handy-dandy chart to help you gauge which antics are easy and budget-friendly, which require a trip to the store, and which ones demand a greater time investment for setup or cleanup. This chart provides a quick snapshot of the effort, planning, and cost involved for each antic. Here's what the check marks indicate:

Easy Breezy

These antics take minimal time to set up and clean up – under 5 minutes! Most families will already have the materials on hand (or they can be easily substituted with similar items from around the house), so there's nothing extra to buy. Just double-check your supplies to avoid surprises!

Plan & Prep Ahead

Antics in this category typically require a special purchase or more time to execute – sometimes both! The materials won't break the bank, but it's a good idea to prepare in advance to ensure you have everything ready.

Can Get Pricey

These antics require materials that will likely cost more than $10 if you need to purchase them. Substitutions may be difficult because of the specialized items needed. Sometimes this higher price tag is due to gifts involved or simply the quantity of materials required.

Occasionally, you might spot a check mark in both the *Plan & Prep Ahead* and *Can Get Pricey* columns. This means the antic will take at least 10 minutes to set up and will likely cost over $10 if you need to buy most of the materials. Always consider what materials you already have on hand and your overall budget for the elf season. Sometimes you may want to substitute an antic with a more budget-friendly one.

Following the charts, you'll find detailed descriptions for each antic, including materials and directions to pull them off. The antics in this book are all listed in alphabetical order by their title.

Ready to dive in? Game on!

Here's What To Expect

This chart provides a snapshot of the amount of effort, planning, and cost involved for each antic in this book. If you see a check mark in a column, that means:

Easy Breezy - the antic should take less than 5 minutes to set up, but verify materials.
Plan & Prep Ahead - you may need to buy some unusual materials ahead of time and/or spend at least 10 minutes setting everything up.
Can Get Pricey - this antic could get expensive if you don't already have most of the main materials.

	Easy Breezy	Plan & Prep Ahead	Can Get Pricey
All Aboard the Shoe Shoe Train	✔		
Animatronic Band	✔		✔
Arrival 1: Introducing…Me!			✔
Arrival 2: Floating By and Dropping In		✔	
Arrival 3: Billboard		✔	
Arrival 4: Can You Tell Who's Back?		✔	
Arrival 5: Balloon Cascade		✔	
Bakery Shop		✔	✔
The Bowl of Champions		✔	
Bowling for Root Beer		✔	✔
Breakfast is Served		✔	
Breakfast To Go	✔		
Brownies	✔	✔	
Bubble Bath	✔		
Candy Cane Choo Choo		✔	
Charmin Snowflakes		✔	
Chicken Wing, Chicken Wing		✔	✔
Christmas Countdown		✔	
Chow Time	✔		
Coat Closet Rave		✔	✔
Despicable Bananas	✔		
Dinosaur Follow the Leader	✔		
Doggone It!		✔	
Duty Calls		✔	
Feeding the Ducks	✔		
Finder's Keepers		✔	
Fish in the Hole!			✔
Floor is Lava			✔
Flour Angel	✔		
Flying Gumballs		✔	

	Easy Breezy	Plan & Prep Ahead	Can Get Pricey
Frisbee Fun	✓		
Game Night		✓	
Games for the Little Ones			✓
Ginger + Bread = Gingerbread House	✓		
Green Thumb		✓	✓
Grow a Tree		✓	
Home Defense		✓	
Homework Helper		✓	
I See London	✓		
I'm a Little Tied Up Right Now	✓		
Indoor Snowman		✓	
Ironing Out a Few Wrinkles	✓		
Just Throw Your Kid's Underwear on the Tree and Call It a Day	✓		
Let's Play Chess			✓
Magic Milk	✓		
Make Room for Candy!		✓	✓
Marshmallow Tic-Tac-Toe	✓		
Naughty! Naughty!	✓		
Nutcracker Studio			✓
O' Chipmus Tree		✓	✓
On-Call Mechanic		✓	
Orange You Glad It's Morning?	✓		
Out of This World Delivery Backups	✓		✓
The Parfect Hiding Spot	✓		✓
Perfectly Physics	✓		
PicELFso		✓	✓
Popcorn Palooza		✓	
Potty Songs		✓	✓
Rain Cloud	✓		
Rainbow Maker		✓	
Reindeer Lessons		✓	
Reindeer Training Academy			✓
Remote Controlled Fun	✓		
Retribution		✓	✓
Roasted Elf		✓	✓
Rockin' Around the Cactus Tree			✓
Sack Races	✓		

	Easy Breezy	Plan & Prep Ahead	Can Get Pricey
Scavenger Hunt #1: Seek and Find		✔	
Scavenger Hunt #2: Riddle Me This		✔	
Shoeshine		✔	
Silly String Battle		✔	
Singing for Santa		✔	
Sippy Straw		✔	
Snowball Catapult Fight		✔	
Snowflakes	✔		
Sticky Wipe	✔		
Stockings Filled With... Underwear?!?	✔		
Storage Room Shoot Out		✔	
Story Time for Toys	✔		
Stuck in the Claw Machine			✔
Taste Test	✔		
Toilet Bowl Toothbrush	✔		
TP Patrol	✔		
TP'd Tree	✔		
Underwear Hang Gliding	✔		
Vertical Blinds		✔	
Vitamins Help Candy Canes Grow		✔	
Vroom Vroom Snowman	✔		
Washing Day			✔
What a Bowtiful Smile!	✔		
Whirligig		✔	
Worst Christmas Cookies Ever!	✔		
You'll Never Guess What This Gift Is!		✔	

ALL ABOARD THE SHOE SHOE TRAIN

You say "choo choo," I say "shoe shoe." Whatever your language, hop onboard and have some fun!

Here's what you'll need:

→ All the shoes your kid owns (add other family members' shoes to the train if you don't have at least 6 shoes)

→ One toy figurine or stuffed animal to fit in each shoe.

Set it up:

1. Line the shoes up one after the other, like train cars.
2. Place your family's elf in the first shoe, as the train engineer.
3. Position the other figurines in the remaining shoes.
4. Add a sign, such as "ALL ABOARD THE SHOE SHOE TRAIN!"

Want to make it even more fun?

⭐ Position the shoes on a train track instead of the floor.

⭐ Place Christmas decorations and figurines in each shoe instead of toy figurines.

ANIMATRONIC BAND

Gather up all of those animatronics you've collected over the different holidays because it's time for a very special performance.

Here's what you'll need:

→ At least 3 different animated figures that move and play music
→ Other stuffed animals, figurines, and kid-sized instruments

Set it up:

1. Arrange the animatronics as if they're in a band and playing a concert.
2. Position the remainder of the figurines as audience members facing the musicians.

Want to make it even more fun?

⭐ Add a projector or strobe light.
⭐ Add a microphone so your kid can sing along.

Where to Shop?

CVS and Walgreens often sell animatronic holiday figures in their seasonal aisle.

ARRIVAL #1 INTRODUCING...ME!

"Make yourself at home," you say? Don't mind if I do!

Here's what you'll need:

→ Elf-sized furnishings, including a miniature elf-sized Christmas tree

Set it up:

1. The first year your elf visits, this can be Day 1's antic, with nothing else planned. But in the years after that, the room should be in addition to whatever's planned for your elf's arrival.

2. Purchase (or, if you're feeling a little crafty, build) a room's worth of elf-sized furnishings that can be displayed throughout the elf season. Picture a cozy little reading nook where your elf can chill out and relax from all that mischief-making: rocking chair, side table, door, rug, book, lamp...maybe even a nice cup of hot cocoa.

3. Once your kids have found their elf in the morning, he has a retreat for anytime he wants a little peace and quiet before he returns to the North Pole.

Want to make it even more fun?

⭐ Your elf can host visitors throughout the day. Simply "invite" another toy to join him in the room at various times over the course of the day when your little one isn't looking. On Story Day, I have a book that I read to my miniature toy visitors.

⭐ Move your elf's room to different locations around the house each year he visits.

⭐ Periodically change up the snacks on your elf's side table.

⭐ Place really tiny gifts under the tree that your kids can open.

⭐ For older kids, you can post an "eviction" notice on the elf's door on December 23rd for nonpayment of rent.

Where to Shop?
Everything pictured here, including the decorated Christmas tree, was purchased as one set on Etsy since my family isn't too crafty. I reuse it every year.

ARRIVAL #2 – FLOATING BY AND DROPPING IN

I was just floating by the neighborhood and thought I'd drop in...

Here's what you'll need:

→ 6 or more balloons filled with helium and tied together as a balloon bouquet – the more balloons the better (your elf might weigh down the bouquet)

→ A marker

Set it up:

1. Tie your elf to the balloon bouquet, or, if you have the budget for it, buy a balloon with your elf placed inside of it.

2. Write a message on some of the balloons, such as:

   - I love (your kid's name)
   - Direct from the North Pole!
   - Ready to have some fun?
   - Ho, ho, ho! Time for a show!

Where to Shop?

A dollar store is probably the least expensive place to buy helium balloons. Or you can buy a helium tank at a party shop and fill your own.

Want to make it even more fun?

⭐ Place the elf in a small wicker basket and attach it to the balloon bouquet (an old Easter basket might also work).

⭐ Have the elf deliver a special letter from Santa.

ARRIVAL #3 – BILLBOARD

Can you guess who's arrived?!?

Here's what you'll need:

➜ Print out a HUGE announcement message: I printed one letter per colored sheet of paper

➜ Christmas-themed window and door decorations

➜ Stick-on hooks and tape

➜ Candy canes

➜ Optional: dollar store Christmas necklace, beard, and/or hat

Set it up:

1. Decide on a message to announce the family elf's arrival and print it out ahead of time. The bigger, the better!

2. If you're going to use stick-on hooks for your decorations, keep in mind that most need to be positioned at least a half hour before you plan on using them.

3. Post the message on a wall that your kids will immediately see when they exit their bedroom or the hallway.

4. Deck out the room with various holiday decorations – the tackier, the better!

5. Hang candy canes or streamers on the tv, ceiling fan blades, and/or door handles.

Want to make it even more fun?

⭐ Create other signs to post on the walls around the house with motivational Christmas slogans and cheers.

⭐ Create "Wanted" posters for Christmas fun, using a picture of your kid.

Where to Shop?

A dollar store is your best bet for this antic, as they sell a variety of large holiday decorations and holiday attire on the cheap.

ARRIVAL #4 – CAN YOU TELL WHO'S BACK?

Look around and see if you can guess who's just returned for another elf-tastic season!

Here's what you'll need:

- → Print out about 300 or so color "portraits" of your family's elf
- → Tape to affix the pictures to the walls
- → Streamers

Set it up:

1. Choose a room that your kid will immediately see upon exiting his/her bedroom or when exiting a hallway/stairwell.
2. Tape the portrait pictures all over the room.
3. Hang streamers across the outside of your child's bedroom door.
4. Position your family's elf to hold the tape.

Want to make it even more fun?

- ⭐ If you have a lot of time on your hands, decorate the entire house with portraits of your family's elf.
- ⭐ Alternate pictures of your family's elf with pictures of your kid.
- ⭐ Instead of posting the pictures throughout a room, choose 1 wall and completely "wallpaper" it with all of the portraits.

ARRIVAL #5 – BALLOON CASCADE

Who doesn't love to open their bedroom door only to be greeted by a mountain of cascading balloons? Talk about a surprise!

Here's what you'll need:

→ Tape that can stand up to some weight

→ A big sheet of plastic that's wider than the doorframe

→ 30+ colored balloons

Set it up:

1. Blow up all the balloons. Do not use helium because you want the balloons to drop down on your kid when he/she opens the door, not rise up to the ceiling. It's best to blow up the balloons earlier in the day and then store them in some garbage bags.

2. Once your kid has gone to sleep, tape the left side of the plastic sheet to the left side of the outside doorframe of your kid's room.

3. Stretch the plastic to the other side of the door (but leave some space for the balloons to fit in) and tape it to the right side of the doorframe.

4. Pull the bottom of the plastic sheet tight and tape it to both sides of the doorframe so no balloons can escape. Essentially, you're trying to create a pocket with enough slack at the top and middle to fit a lot of balloons but then it's tight at the bottom so the balloons don't fall out.

5. Do not tape anything to the door itself – just the outside door frame.

6. Fill the pocket you created with the balloons.

7. Make sure to use tape that's strong enough to hold the pocket throughout the night without damaging the paint/drywall. It doesn't really matter how ugly it looks on the outside of the door because that's not what your kid will see when the door initially opens (and elf-work isn't always picture perfect, anyways).

8. Position your family's elf somewhere else in the house. That year I stuck with the balloon theme and rode my hot air balloon near the living room.

9. Caution – Do not use this antic with little ones, due to potential suffocation hazards. Wait until your kid is old enough to know how to safely tear down the plastic. You'll want to be there anyways to record your kid's surprised reaction.

Want to make it even more fun?

⭐ Sometimes it's hard to improve on what's already great. My family's kid still talks about this antic nearly 10 years later.

BAKERY SHOP

Sweet treats for sweet kids are always on the menu at the Elf Bakery!

Here's what you'll need:

➜ Mini decorated cookie treats
➜ Mini apron and baking gear
➜ Mini bag of frosting

Set it up:

1. Place the apron on your family's elf and arrange him on a shelf or counter (away from nosy and hungry pets).
2. Position the cookies, baking gear, and mini treats around the elf.

Want to make it even more fun?

⭐ Have some cookie baking ingredients nearby so your kid can make some cookies later in the day.

⭐ Set up the scene to make it look like your family's elf spent the whole night making the cookies – flour and sprinkles all over, frosting spread on the edge of the kitchen sink, bowls, spoons, and cookie cutters spread throughout the kitchen, a tall pile of dishes in the sink – you know, just your typical overall epic mess.

Where to Shop?

You can make your own cookies or purchase them. All of the cookies and setup materials here were purchased on Etsy.

Make or purchase an elf cookie with your child's name on it.

THE BOWL OF CHAMPIONS

They say that breakfast is the most important meal of the day, so why not serve more of it? I'm thinking a REALLY big bowl – you know, that one you already use several times a day?!?

Here's what you'll need:

➜ A clean toilet – you're going to be getting really close and personal with this thing, so disinfect it before getting started

➜ A full roll of plastic wrap that clings really well and will hold up to some weight on top of it

➜ A HUGE economy-sized box of multi-colored cereal (or 2 to 3 normal sized boxes) – go with the generic and cheapest cereal you can find because it won't be eaten

➜ The largest spoon you have on hand

Set it up:

1. Flip up the toilet seat.

2. You don't want to just pour cereal into the hole because (A) it would take A LOT more cereal to fill it up to the top than you think it will and (B) you'll clog your toilet if you try to flush it all down the drain when the stunt's over (and, ewww, who wants to scoop out stuff from the family toilet?!?).

3. Tear off several pieces of plastic wrap that extend all the way across the top of the hole and then another 3 inches or so beyond it on each side. The idea is to completely seal over the hole so you can pour cereal on top of it without the plastic wrap sinking into the water in the bottom of the bowl. Don't worry if you see plastic around the sides. Your kids probably won't even notice, and if they do, they won't care.

4. Now's the time to make sure the plastic wrap is really secure across the sides of the bowl by running your hands over it.

5. Place the toilet seat down on the bowl and then carefully start to pour the cereal on top of the plastic inside the seat, watching carefully to ensure the plastic stays put. Pour enough cereal for it to mound up a bit.

6. Gently place the spoon on top of the cereal in the bowl, resting it on the toilet seat.

7. A note from your elf works well here. Mine said: IT WUZ THU BIGGIST BOLE I CUD FIND. DIG IN!

8. It should go without saying, but just in case…DON'T let your child eat this cereal. That could result in the gift that keeps on giving – and no one wants that particular experience!

Want to make it even more fun?

⭐ Make another bowl for your elf by filling up the nearby sink with cereal and then position him "eating" it with his own spoon.

⭐ Make an even larger bowl by filling up the bathtub with cereal. The advantage to this is you don't have to use plastic wrap. The disadvantage to this is you'll probably have to break into your child's college fund to afford the cereal it would take to do this.

Where to Shop?

Come on, do you really need advice for where to buy cheap cereal and plastic wrap?!?

BOWLING FOR ROOT BEER

Let's make a Bowl-a-Rama. Root! Root! Root for a strike! Well, not really, because smashing a bowling ball through some glass bottles would make quite a mess!

Here's what you'll need:

➔ At least 10 bottles of root beer and/or soda, as close to the same size as possible

➔ A bowling ball, or a realistic enough replacement

➔ Optional:

- Bowling shoes
- Scorecard with a pencil nearby
- Mini bowling kit to set up a separate lane

1. Set up your bowling pins on a flat surface. Someone got a little out of control buying different soda flavors at the local BevMo store, so I ended up using 36 bottles for my bowling pins instead of the standard 10 pins. For a traditional (and much less expensive) set up, use 4 rows, like this:

```
*  *  *  *
 *  *  *
  *  *
   *
```

2. Position your elf inside the bowling shoes or on top of the bowling ball.

3. Alternative: Set a few bottles down on the ground in a horizontal position with the ball nearby, as if your elf just attempted to knock down the pins. Show that number on your elf's bowling scorecard for the frame. Be careful if you have pets – all it takes is one curious pooch to nudge the bowling ball into some of the upright bottles and the fizzy soda fireworks will be going off, leaving you with an epic mess to clean up.

4. I set up a separate bowling lane for my military friends, using a mini *Glow and Bowl* kit that was on clearance the previous summer at the local TJ Maxx.

Want to make it even more fun?

- Stage some figurines nearby as spectators to cheer on your elf.
- Print out an old-school bowling score card with your elf's name on it and current score.
- Simulate a disco bowl session by adding music and flashing lights.
- Use juice boxes, soda cans, or bottles of other types of soda. Just try to make sure they're all about the same size.
- My family's kid had fun spending the next month trying each flavor and assigning it a grade on the report card.

Where to Shop?

→ Liquor store chains often carry a large variety of root beer brands and different kinds of soda bottles. I bought mine at BevMo.

→ Mini bowling kits can often be found in the toy section of your local dollar store, and boxed mini kits can also be found at Barnes and Noble and Amazon.

→ Hobby stores carry mini soda bottles in their dollhouse section if you want to duplicate the soda bottles on a smaller scale instead of buying a mini bowling kit.

BREAKFAST IS SERVED!

A balanced breakfast is a very important start to the day. Here's a meal that includes all of an elf's major food groups. Chef's kiss!

Here's what you'll need:

- → Plain spaghetti, cooked
- → 1 can of whipped cream
- → Marshmallows
- → Maple syrup
- → Bag of Sugar
- → Sprinkles – at least 3 different kinds

Set it up:

1. Mound the spaghetti on the plate.
2. Squirt on some whipped cream.
3. Add some sprinkles and marshmallows.
4. Top with some maple syrup and sugar.
5. Stick a fork in it and dig in!
6. If it's not as sweet as your kid's liking, you can always add on 16 dollops of frosting.

Want to make it even more fun?

⭐ Instead of serving this at the breakfast table, put in on a tv tray right outside your kid's bedroom door, along with a vase of flowers. Voila! Breakfast in bed!

⭐ Provide this recipe for a nutritious elf smoothie that your kid can make: Put 5 scoops of ice cream in a blender. Add 2 cups of white sugar, 1 ½ cups of corn syrup, and 1 cup of brown sugar. Add ½ of a small strawberry. Blend and enjoy. Makes 1 serving.

BREAKFAST TO GO

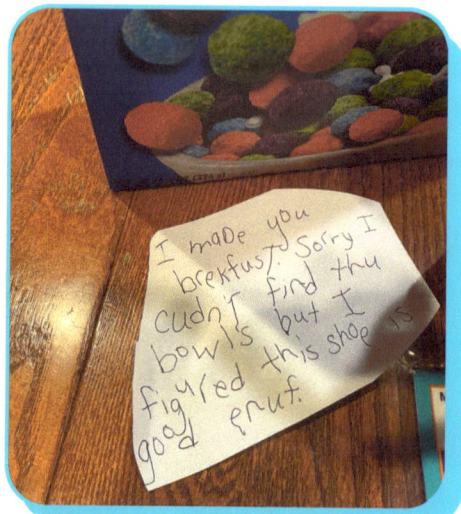

Eating on the run? I have a solution!

Here's what you'll need:

→ Save one of your kid's used shoes that he/she has recently grown out of (preferably one that is in such poor shape it can't be donated for reuse)

→ Cereal

→ Spoon

→ A few candy canes and hard candy pieces

→ Syrup

Set it up:

1. Pour the cereal into the shoe.

2. Position the candy canes in the cereal and place a few hard candy pieces on top.

3. Stick the spoon in the cereal.

4. Set the cereal box and syrup nearby.

5. Position your family's elf so he's peeking out of the cereal box.

6. Leave a note. Here's what I wrote on mine: "I made you brekfust. Sorry I cudn't find thu bowls but I figured this shoe is good enuf."

Want to make it even more fun?

⭐ Use Dad's shoe instead of the Kid's.

⭐ Use a few cans of Spaghetti Os instead of cereal for lunch on the go.

⭐ Instead of cereal, fill the shoe up with sprinkles.

BROWNEEZ

Think of how excited your kid will be to open up the oven door for some brownEEz!

Here's what you'll need:

→ A cookie sheet
→ White paper
→ Brown markers, crayons, and/or colored pencils

Set it up:

1. Write various styles and sizes of a capital and lowercase letter E on white paper.
2. Color them different shades of brown and then cut them out.
3. Repeat steps 1-2 for about 12 total.
4. Arrange the Es on the cookie sheet on a rack in the oven. Do NOT turn the oven on.
5. Leave a note for your kid similar to this: "I baykd sum brownEEz for you. Thay r in thu uven."

Want to make it even more fun?

⭐ Make a mess on the countertop with bowls, cooking utensils, cocoa, and flour, as if the elf was mixing up brownies.

BUBBLE BATH

Even elves need to have a little "me time."

Here's what you'll need:

➜ 1 bag mini marshmallows
➜ One or more rubber duckies

Set it up:

1. Close the drain on the sink.
2. Pour the mini marshmallows into the sink.
3. Place your family's elf so he's leaning back and relaxing.
4. Add a few rubber ducks to float on top.

Want to make it even more fun?

⭐ Make it a bubbling jacuzzi and replace the rubber ducks with a few Barbie dolls or other elves as friends.

CANDY CANE CHOO CHOO

Gather up your friends because it's all aboard to Funville!

Here's what you'll need:

→ 1 train set with 5-10 cars and track (select open cars and platform cars)

→ Mini candy canes and/or peppermint puffs

→ Mini toy figurines

→ Small Christmas figurines (nutcrackers, Christmas tree, snowman)

Set it up:

1. Set up the train tracks and place the train engine and cars on it.

2. Position some toy figurines in each car.

3. Place the candy canes in one of the cars.

4. Turn it on when your kid wakes up.

Want to make it even more fun?

⭐ "Tie" another figurine (or your elf) to the track and have a villain stand nearby (just don't turn on the train)

Where to Shop?

Most of these trains were purchased at Walmart and independent toy stores.

CHARMIN SNOWFLAKES

No paper is safe from an elf's snowflake scissors!

Here's what you'll need:

→ 1 roll of toilet paper
→ A good, sharp pair of scissors

Set it up:

1. Gently unroll about 8 to 10 squares of toilet paper without tearing them off from the roll. You don't want too many squares, otherwise they'll be too thick for the scissors to cut through.

2. Fold the squares together, and then fold that square as you would to cut out snowflake designs.

3. Cut out some shapes to make a snowflake pattern.

4. Gently unroll the squares so they hang down from the roll.

5. Set your family's elf on top of the roll, along with a child-safe pair of scissors.

Want to make it even more fun?

⭐ Make it a snowflake party by having other stuffed animals cut their own designs of snowflakes.

⭐ Hang sheets of snowflake toilet paper from the doorway.

CHICKEN WING, CHICKEN WING...

Have you heard this song that's sweeping the nation?

Chicken wing, chicken wing,

Hot dog and baloney,

Chicken and macaroni,

Chillin' with my homies!

Why not recreate it in your family's refrigerator?

Here's what you'll need:

→ 2 chicken wings (fried looks best for this)

→ A package of hot dogs (or just use one hot dog in a bun)

→ A package of bologna

→ A few chicken nuggets (any kind of chicken works, including a whole one)

→ Uncooked macaroni pieces (or a package of mac n cheese)

→ Small toy figurines

→ Write each line of the song above on a piece of paper

Want to make it even more fun?

★ Have a recording of the song ready to go when your child opens the fridge door.

★ Write each word of the song on a piece of paper and leave a paper trail (with the words of the song in order) that leads to the refrigerator.

Set it up:

1. Don't try to do this the day after you just went grocery shopping. You want your fridge to be fairly empty.
2. Clear off 4 shelves in your refrigerator (or just do what I did, and push everything to the back of the shelf).
3. Position 2 chicken wings on the top shelf.
4. Stage the hot dog (or package of hot dogs) and the package of bologna on the next shelf.
5. Set the plate of chicken nuggets and macaroni on the shelf under the bologna.
6. Position the toy figurines next to your family elf on the bottom shelf.
7. Tape the papers with each line of the song on the corresponding shelf.
8. You may want to leave some kind of hint when your kid wakes up so he/she knows to look in the refrigerator.

CHRISTMAS COUNTDOWN

North Pole sticks to a very tight timetable to get all toys made and delivered on time. So elves always know EXACTLY how many days are left until the big day! I use a Christmas countdown with my family to build even more anticipation and excitement for Santa's arrival.

Here's what you'll need:

→ Mini sticky notes in a variety of colors

→ Marker

Set it up:

1. Decide on what you want your Christmas Countdown message to say. Write 1 letter per sticky note and alternate colors for each of the words in the message.

2. Post the sticky notes on a mirror.

Want to make it even more fun?

⭐ Post Christmas riddles instead of a countdown with the question on one mirror and the answer posted somewhere else in the house.

CHOW TIME

Elves can think of very creative ways to get the job done. Take, for example, feeding the pets their kibble. I use a whole construction crew to make sure our pets get their chow delivered on time so it's fresh and nutritious.

Here's what you'll need:

→ Toy bulldozer and other construction equipment

→ A few toy construction figurines

→ Bag of dry pet food

Set it up:

1. Position your family's elf on the bulldozer next to your pet's food bowl and fill its bucket with dry kibble.

2. Position the construction figurines and equipment nearby.

Want to make it even more fun?

⭐ Make a long assembly line of dump trucks, wagons, and other vehicles that can hold dry pet food leading from the bag to the pet dish.

COAT CLOSET RAVE

Party in the house!!! Did you know that some elves have a little side hustle going on as DJs? There's no better way to work off those Christmas cookies than shaking your bootie!

Here's what you'll need:

- → glow sticks
- → LED light up tubes, spinners, and necklaces
- → foil
- → small matchbox-sized box
- → a round, black quarter-sized magnet (or any object that looks like that)
- → white paper or cardstock
- → black marker
- → small Bluetooth speaker or other type of device with speaker

Set it up:

1. Take everything out of your coat closet and pile it around the area, making it look like the elf just randomly threw everything out.
2. Draw a mask that looks like the one "Marshmello" DJ wears and secure it on your elf.
3. Wrap the foil around the box and glue the black round magnet to the box as if it's a turntable. Position the elf in the closet and set the "turntable" on his lap.
4. Position some stuffed animals and figurines as if they're dancing and hang some of the glow sticks and LED items on and around them.
5. Set the speaker on a shelf in a closet so it plays music that's loud enough to hear when you're a room or two away.
6. Close the closet door and let the party begin.

Want to make it even more fun?

- ⭐ Project a black light in the closet (or provide a black light flashlight) and post papers with messages on them that can only be seen in the blacklight.
- ⭐ Hang a spinning disco ball from the closet rod.
- ⭐ Use a projector light in the closet.

Where to Shop?

- → Target often sells bulk glow sticks for Halloween, so you can sometimes snag them on clearance on the days after.
- → Amazon sells a wide selection of LED party toys.

DESPICABLE BANANAS

You don't have to stop at just decorating the Christmas tree – bananas provide the perfect canvas for some despicable friends.

Here's what you'll need:

→ A bunch of bananas that are just ripe – you don't want any large black spots on them

→ A Sharpie marker

Set it up:

1. Draw a Despicable-Me Minion on each banana and set your family's elf nearby, holding the marker.

Want to make it even more fun?

★ Draw different kinds of faces or Christmas decorations instead of minions.

★ Instead of having the elf draw the characters, place a Minion figurine next to the bananas, holding the marker while the elf watches.

DINOSAUR FOLLOW THE LEADER

Gather up all your dino pals for a mini parade!

Here's what you'll need:

→ 1 tall/large dinosaur figurine and several small ones

Set it up:

1. Make a single line out of the dinosaurs and place the tall dinosaur at the front, as if it's leading the others.
2. Position your family's elf on top of the tall dinosaur, as if he's riding it like a horse.

Want to make it even more fun?

⭐ This works for any kind of toy: Cars, stuffed animals, etc. and is best done the first year your elf visits when your kid is very young.

DOGGONE IT!

Dogs are an occupational hazard for elves, so it's important to stay on their good side. But dog slobber is the worst! So I use my handy-dandy treat launcher. Just aim, shoot, and then close the door behind you so you can move on to working a little elf magic around the house!

Here's what you'll need:

→ 1 handheld battery-operated treat launcher

→ Container/pouch of your pet's favorite treats

→ Stuffed/toy dogs - any variety works

Set it up:

1. Position your elf on a table or counter.
2. Load some treats in the treat launcher and arrange a few extras nearby the elf.
Leave the pouch close by as well.
3. Position the dogs as if they're begging for treats, placing a few treats nearby them.

Want to make it even more fun?

⭐ If you can't find a treat launcher or don't want to buy one, substitute a slingshot (homemade or one you have around the house). The idea is the same.

Where to Shop?

Treat launchers are often found in the cheap holiday gift sections at CVS and Walgreens. I bought this one at Walgreens for a few bucks.

DUTY CALLS

It's US against THEM in an epic battle. Bring your family's favorite military video game to life with the help of a video game controller and some of the military's finest (action figures).

Here's what you'll need:

→ Video game controller
→ LOTS of military soldier figurines
→ Toy tanks, trucks, and armored vehicles
→ Nerf bullets

Set it up:

1. The idea of this antic is to make it look like your family's elf is bringing a military video game to life. The soldiers "in" the video game are shooting Nerf bullets out of the tv as they fight against the soldiers positioned around the elf.

2. Position the elf with the video game controller, looking at the tv, as if he's playing the game.

3. Stage the soldiers in various offensive positions to make it look like they're engaging in fierce battle with the characters in the video game. Arrange the toy tanks, trucks, and vehicles around them.

4. Throw a bunch of Nerf bullets around so this looks like an epic battleground. Remember: Messier is ALWAYS better for any antic!

Where to Shop?

Second-hand stores sometimes sell bags of action figurines, but it's hit and miss.

It's best to use the figurines you already have on hand around the house.

Want to make it even more fun?

⭐ If you were planning on buying a new release of the game for Christmas anyways, you could upload it and have your family's elf playing it when your kids wake up as an early gift.

⭐ Dress your family's elf in military fatigues.

⭐ Set up a WWI-style trench out of Lincoln Logs, Legos, or jacks in front of the action figures.

FEEDING THE DUCKS

Feeling a little lazy? There's nothing easier than dumping some rubber ducks into a bathtub to create a delightful scene!

Here's what you'll need:

→ A slice or two of bread
→ Some rubber ducks

Where to Shop?

It's not worth the expense of buying ducks just for this activity, but, if you feel you must, try Oriental Trading Company or Amazon to buy rubber ducks in bulk.

Set it up:

1. Fill up a tub with some water.
2. Throw some rubber ducks in the tub. As you can see, my family has TONS of rubber ducks that they got from claw machines and give aways. Don't feel like you need to have this many. Three or four will do just fine.
3. Position your elf, placing the bread nearby. Tear off a corner or two of the bread as if your elf has been feeding the ducks. Eat those pieces or just throw them away.
4. Call it a night.

Want to make it even more fun?

★ Don't. Enjoy some time for yourself instead.

FINDER'S KEEPERS

There's treasure to be found in them hills! Well...maybe since we're in the house it's under plastic cups instead of hills.

Here's what you'll need:

→   50 or more red plastic cups (or any color, as long as they're not clear)

→   The same number of candy canes, your child's favorite candy, or dollar bills as there are number of days left until Christmas

→   A note saying "There are (insert the number) days until Christmas. I've hidden (insert the same number) of candy canes in these cups. Can you find them?"

Set it up:

1.   Position the cups upside down all over the floor of the room.

2.   Place one candy cane under one of the cups. Repeat this for the remaining number of candy canes you have.

3.   Leave the note on the floor just outside of your kid's room.

Want to make it even more fun?

⭐   Instead of placing all the cups in just one room, place them all around the house.

⭐   Set a challenge of finding all the candy canes without picking up more than 25 empty cups.

FISH IN THE HOLE!

Why play cornhole with beanbags with bags of candy work just as well?

Here's what you'll need:

➜ 2 or 3 bags of Swedish Fish (or use fireballs for a game of "Fire in the Hole")

➜ 1 cornhole board

Set it up:

1. Seat your elf on a tv tray, side table, or shelf.

2. Set the cornhole board on the ground an appropriate length away.

3. Place the bags of Swedish fish on and around the cornhole board as if your elf was throwing them.

4. During this Christmas season I left a note each day with a riff on the lyrics to the 12 Days of Christmas song. For this antic, I wrote: "On thu therd day of kristmus my tru luv gav to me a cornhol game plade with littl fishees!"

Want to make it even more fun?

⭐ Use real bags of beans instead of the Swedish Fish. Ensure that one "breaks" so that beans fly all over the floor.

⭐ Have your elf "throw" real ears of corn (either fresh or those found in the frozen foods section at the grocer) instead of the Swedish Fish.

FLOOR IS LAVA

All right, who let the volcanoes in the house?!?

Here's what you'll need:

→ 1 set of special "lava-proof shoes"

→ A roll or two of red crepe streamer

→ Any kind of flying contraption for your family's elf, like a hot air balloon, airplane, or blimp

→ Fishing line

Set it up:

1. Position the fishing line so you can hang up the family elf's flying contraption.

2. Position the elf in it.

3. Set the special lava-proof shoes next to your kid's bedroom door.

4. Tear off strips of the red crepe streamer and position them around the room and up to wherever the elf is hanging to mimic lava waves.

5. Leave a note to help explain the situation. Here's the one I left: "BE CAREFUL! FLOOR IS LAVA! WEAR THESE SPECIAL SHOES."

Want to make it even more fun?

⭐ Provide safe dots for your kid to jump to instead of buying special shoes to make this a little more active.

⭐ If you really want to get elaborate, place strings of red lights on the floor and cover with red plastic tablecloths (like those sold at Party City). Set "safe" circles around the path for your kid to jump to.

Where to Shop?

→ Find shoes like this at a dollar store or Walmart.

→ This flying balloon Calico Critters Sky Ride Adventure was purchased at Homegoods.

→ Crepe paper streamers can be purchased at party stores and craft stores.

FLOUR ANGEL

Here's the indoor version of a snow angel.

Here's what you'll need:

→ A bag of flour

→ Optional: A cutting board to minimize the mess

Set it up:

1. Pour some flour onto the counter or cutting board and create a snow angel pattern on it.
2. Set your family's elf on top.

Want to make it even more fun?

⭐ Use sprinkles or confetti instead of flour.

FLYING GUMBALLS

Who will score the most points getting the gumballs in each pot?

Here's what you'll need:

➔ Two measuring spoons: I used a ½ teaspoon and a 1 teaspoon
➔ 2 wide-width rubber bands
➔ About 30 gumballs (or M&Ms, grapes, marbles, Tic Tacs)
➔ 3 or more pots or bowls
➔ 3 or more sticky notes to write point values on
➔ 2 of any kind of 2" tall by 2" wide stabilizers for the spoons to rest on – I constructed mine out of Legos
➔ 1 toy figurine to compete against your elf

Set it up:

1. Attach the rubber band around the stabilizer height-wise and slide the teaspoon under the band so it's balanced on the stabilizer.
2. Place a gumball in each measuring spoon.
3. Position the elf and the toy figurine on the side of the stabilizers that's closest to the spoon handle, as if they're going to reach out their hand and bang down the spoon handle.
4. Position the bag/box/bowl of gumballs next to them so they can reload.
5. Set the 3 pots/bowls varying distances away in front of the elf and figurine.
6. Label the pot/bowl closest to them as 5 points, the next closest one as 10 points, and the farthest one away as 25 points.
7. Place a few gumballs in each pot/bowl and scatter gumballs around the floor.

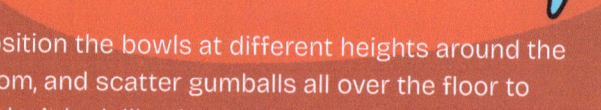

Want to make it even more fun?

⭐ Position the bowls at different heights around the room, and scatter gumballs all over the floor to make it look like the gumballs were flying all around.

⭐ Affix mini mallets to the hands of the elf and toy figurine.

⭐ Use tiny rubber chickens instead of gumballs (you can buy 12-packs of them on Amazon).

FRISBEE FUN

What dog doesn't like to play fetch?

Here's what you'll need:

- A large bag of tortillas
- Toy dog

Set it up:

1. Position your elf on a table or ledge, sitting next to an open bag of tortillas.
2. Position the dog on the floor, next to a piece of tortilla, as if it was eating it.
3. Position tortillas all over the floor, as if the elf was trying to throw frisbees for the dog to fetch.
4. I left this note: I SEE YER MOM BOT SUM FRISBEES. I'M TEECHING SLEENKY DOG HOW TO FETCH. IT'S NOT TERNING OUT SO GOOD.

Want to make it even more fun?

- Have the elf gift your child a real frisbee.

GAME NIGHT

Calling all stuffed animals and figurines! It's time to get your game on! Everyone has their favorite board games, so why not host a simultaneous competition? That's right: it's time to set up every single game you own and make this a game night to remember.

Here's what you'll need:

➔ A variety of board and card games – the more the better. The idea is to cover up as much surface space of the room with games as possible.

➔ About 3 to 4 figurines/stuffed animals per game

Set it up:

1. This is easy but time consuming. Set up each game to make it look like it's realistically being played by the action figurines and stuffed animals.

2. It's a good idea to space out each game, so the pieces don't get mixed up with another game during clean up.

3. Remember: The more games you set up, the more visually impressive this antic is. But if you don't want to set up every game you have, think about leaving a pile of game boxes that the action figurines and stuffed animals have rejected.

4. Save this antic for older kids because then you can leave them with the monumental task of cleaning up while you enjoy a well-deserved cup of coffee!

Want to make it even more fun?

⭐ If your child has been wanting a new board game, position your elf next to the unopened box.

⭐ If you have Scrabble or Hangman, spell out some funny words.

GAMES FOR THE LITTLE ONES

There's nothing like a little friendly competition among pals!

Here's what you'll need:

→ 5 or 6 miniature games like Connect 4, Hungry, Hungry, Hippo, Air Hockey, and Tic Tac Toe

→ Very small stuffed animals and/or toy figurines

→ Mini trophy

Set it up:

1. This one's easy. Simply position the stuffed animals and figurines as if they're playing the various games.

2. Place the trophy nearby for one of the animals to win.

Want to make it even more fun?

⭐ Add in a new mini battery-operated arcade game for your kid like Pac Man or Frogger.

⭐ Include a mini version of your kid's favorite board game.

⭐ Make a mini poster that ranks the different players, showing how many games they've won so far.

Where to Shop?

→ The Tic-Tac-Toe game and air hockey table pictured here were both purchased at a dollar store.

→ The mini Hungry, Hungry Hippo game and pinball set were purchased at Cracker Barrel, but Amazon also sells the "World's Smallest" series of toys and games.

→ The mini Connect 4 and iPad were purchased on Etsy.

→ Mini arcade games are sold at Target and Walmart, as well as online.

GINGER + BREAD = GINGERBREAD HOUSE

This is the lazy parent's dream. Just arrange a few pieces of bread around a spice jar and you're pretty much done. Sweet! To get the joke, kids will need to have a good understanding of what a typical gingerbread house is.

Here's what you'll need:

→ A small plate
→ 3 pieces of bread
→ A container/tin of ginger
→ Optional: Sprinkles

Want to make it even more fun?

⭐ Leave a packaged gingerbread house kit nearby so your kids can make their own.

⭐ For a variation of this, stick four bananas into the sides of a loaf of bread to make "banana bread".

Set it up:

1. You'll be making an A-Frame structure out of the bread.
2. Put one piece of bread on the plate.
3. Set the ginger container on top of it.
4. Position the other two pieces of bread diagonally as the roof so they rest against each other at the top.
5. To make this a bit more colorful, add some sprinkles around the plate.
6. You'll want to leave a note for this one, as some kids may not understand the joke.

GREEN THUMB

As part of the job, elves are required to perpetually wear gloves, so I'm not sure if I actually have a green thumb or not. But since I love making a mess for others to clean up, gardening is right up my alley.

Here's what you'll need:

→ 1/12 scale mini cinder blocks
→ Mini seed packets

Set it up:

1. The idea behind this antic is to construct a raised garden planter.
2. Arrange the blocks so that it looks like your elf is building a raised garden bed.
3. Leave a note. Mine said: TIME TOO MAKE SUM PLANTERS TOO GRO SUM VEJEEO.

Want to make it even more fun?

⭐ Buy some extra blocks and have your elf build a reindeer stall with clippings of grass in it instead of a planter.

⭐ Include a rectangular planter box (about 9 x 24 inches), soil, and seeds for your kids to plant their own veggie garden.

⭐ Leave an avocado seed, some toothpicks, and a clean jar for your child to start an avocado tree. Position 4 toothpicks about a half-inch into the middle diameter of the seed. Set the seed on top of a glass jar - the toothpicks should set on the lip of the jar to stabilize the seed. Fill the jar with water so the bottom ¼" of the seed is in the water, which will encourage roots to grow. Set the jar in a sunny spot and adjust the water each day to make sure the bottom of the seed stays submerged enough for the roots to grow into the water.

Where to Shop?

→ These cement blocks and mini-pallet were purchased on Amazon.
→ The seed packets were found in the dollhouse section of Hobby Lobby.

GROW A TREE

Grow your own Christmas tree in time for Christmas? Count me in!

Here's what you'll need:

→ 1 Amazing Growing Christmas Tree Kit (also called Magic Growing Crystal Christmas Tree)

→ A story book about a Christmas tree that your kids will enjoy listening to or reading themselves – I used Night Tree by Eve Bunting

→ A small group of stuffed animals for your elf to read to

Set it up:

1. Position the elf in a chair with the animals nearby.

2. Prop the book open for your elf to read to the animals.

3. Set the Christmas Tree Kit nearby for your child to work on later in the day.

Want to make it even more fun?

⭐ Instead of the tree kit, buy a live 1-foot-tall Christmas tree in a pot and mini lights and ornaments for your kids to decorate.

⭐ Make your own magic growing trees by conducting a salt crystal experiment on construction paper Christmas tree cutouts. Find directions how by conducting an online search for "kids salt crystal experiment".

Where to Shop?

This Amazing Growing Christmas Tree Kit was purchased at World Market, but Amazon also sells similar kits.

HOME DEFENSE

I can attest that you can rest peacefully knowing that your home is well protected by special forces against security breaches.

Here's what you'll need:

→ Army soldiers

→ Tanks and military vehicles

→ A pillory-type device made out of Legos

→ Two pipe cleaners (or string) to tie your elf's hands together and tie his legs to base of the pillory

Set it up:

1. Construct the pillory. Start by building 2 columns of equal size, each about 2 inches tall, using Legos. Attach the columns to a flat square Lego base, ensuring there is enough space between them for your elf's body to fit.

2. Next, create two smaller columns that are about 1 inch tall and attach them to the tops of the larger columns.

3. Connect the two smaller columns by affixing a rectangular Lego piece at the top.

4. Spell out "HELP" on the Lego base.

5. Position your elf kneeling on the base and tie his legs to the lower columns.

6. Place his head under the top Lego that bridges the two columns, but keep his arms out.

7. Wrap his arms around the outside of the top columns and tie his hands together.

8. Position the army soldiers, tanks, and military vehicles, with guns drawn, around the elf, with some behind a blockade.

9. During this Christmas season I left a note each day with a riff on the lyrics to the 12 Days of Christmas song. For this antic, I wrote: "ON THU FIFTH DAY OF CRISTMUS MY TRU LUV GAV TO ME AN ARMEE THAT THINKS IM INVADING!"

Want to make it even more fun?

✦ No army soldiers in the house? Make it a safari or zoo scene with stuffed animals who want to protect their territory.

✦ Barbies can also hold your elf hostage for a beauty makeover, complete with piles of clothes, makeup, and hair styling products.

HOMEWORK HELPER

 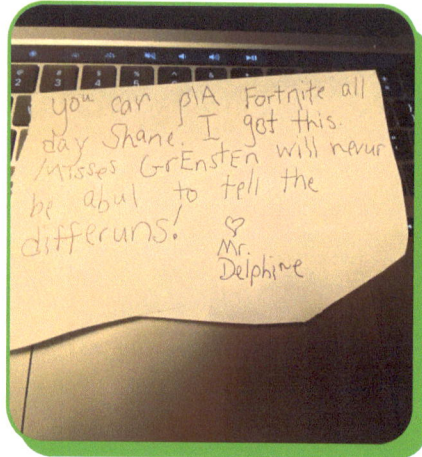 

Want to play video games instead of completing your homework? No problem! I'll make sure your mom and teacher never know!

Here's what you'll need:

→ The following clothes for your kid: A hoodie, a pair of pants, gloves, socks, and shoes
→ Optional: A drop-down face shield left over from work or your COVID pandemic days
→ A roll of paper towels
→ Your kid's laptop or some homework papers and a pencil
→ Lots of newspaper

Want to make it even more fun?

✦ Nope. This is enough work as is.

Set it up:

1. Sweatpants, especially ones with elastic leg cuffs, work well for this. Crumple up the newspaper and stuff it down each leg to fill out the pants as much as possible. Position the pants on a chair or the couch.
2. Zip up the hoodie all the way. Crumple up the newspaper and stuff it in it to fill out the sleeves and body.
3. Position the hoodie on top of the stuffed pants on the chair.
4. Position the arms so they're reaching towards the laptop/homework.
5. Attach the gloves to the arm cuffs of the hoodie.
6. Stuff some newspaper into the socks and then place them in the shoes.
7. Connect the socks to the pants.
8. Stuff a roll of paper towels into the neck of the hoodie a bit so that it still sticks up out of the hoodie at about head-height. Pull the hoodie over the top of the paper towel roll.
9. Position your family's elf into the neck of the hoodie so his head peaks out. If necessary, stuff some newspaper around the paper towel roll to round out the hood a bit.
10. If using it, position the drop-down face shield over the hood so that it covers up the face hole.
11. Turn the laptop on.

I SEE LONDON

What's Christmas without an antic involving underwear?

Here's what you'll need:

→ A ball of string or twine

→ Several clean pairs of each family member's underwear

→ Paper and marker

→ 1 or 2 chip bag clips

→ Optional: Clothespins

Want to make it even more fun?

⭐ Include some elf-sized underwear on the line as well.

Set it up:

1. Make a clothesline to hang the underwear on (I tied the string from one hanging light fixture to another).

2. Hang the pairs of underwear over the string. Or, if you're feeling fancy, attach with clothespins.

3. Make a sign that says: "I see London. I see France. I stole your family's underpants!" and hang it on the clothesline.

4. Position your elf somewhere on the clothesline.

I'M A LITTLE TIED UP RIGHT NOW

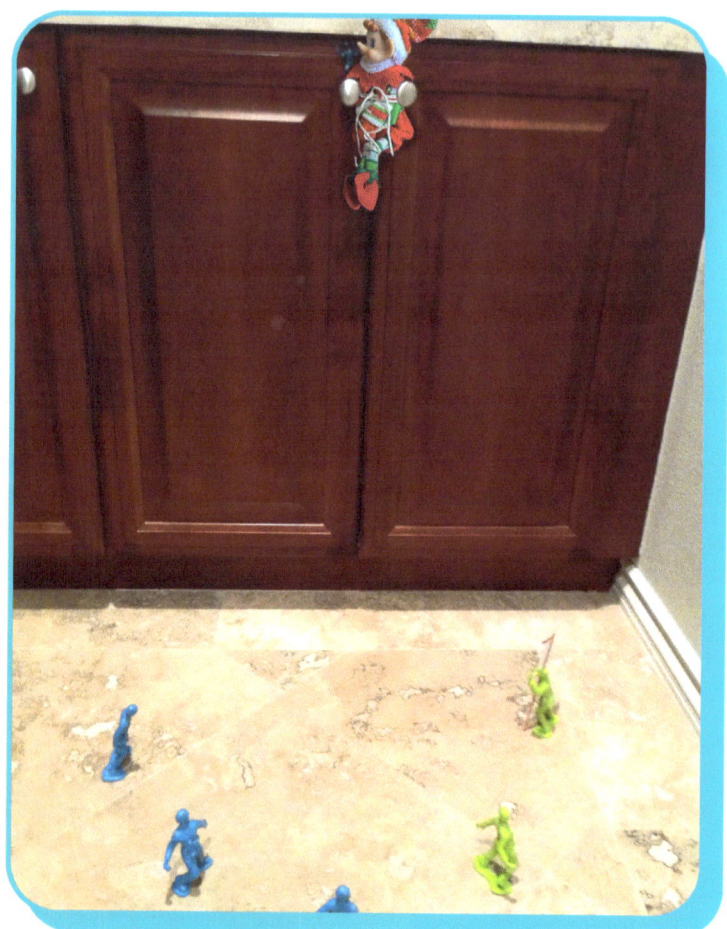

Elves encounter a variety of occupational hazards. Many an elf has dealt with some pretty perilous situations arising from a home's security system.

Here's what you'll need:

→ A ball of string or twine
→ A group of military or action figurines

Set it up:

1. Tie up your elf in a "captured" position and hang him from a cabinet doorknob.
2. Station the figurines around him as if they're guarding him.

Want to make it even more fun?

⭐ Substitute a highway robbery situation instead where the elf is tied up on the ground and a bandit is making off with the elf's mini presents.
⭐ Substitute a Grinch doll for the figurines.

INDOOR SNOWMAN

Snowmen can be built anywhere, as long as they're not Frosty!

Here's what you'll need:

→ 3 rolls of toilet paper

→ 2 wiggly eyes

→ Three 2-inch diameter black circles cut from construction paper for the snowman's buttons

→ Five ¾-inch diameter black circles cut from construction paper for the snowman's mouth

→ Orange triangle cut from construction paper for the snowman's nose

→ Tape

→ Something that can be used as the snowman's scarf

Set it up:

1. Stack the rolls of toilet paper on top of each other.

2. Glue/tape the eyes, nose, and circles for the mouth on the top toilet paper roll.

3. Glue/tape the 3 large circles as the buttons going down the middle and bottom row.

4. Wrap the scarf around where the top and middle toilet paper rolls meet.

5. Place the elf's legs inside the top toilet paper roll or set him nearby.

Want to make it even more fun?

⭐ Make a family of snowmen using paper towel rolls and/or thinner toilet paper rolls (replace the roll when about half of the squares have been used and save the old one for this antic).

IRONING OUT A FEW WRINKLES

This one has certainly made the rounds over the years on Pinterest and with good reason. Who doesn't like an activity involving chips? You're only going to need a handful for this antic. So that leaves plenty for you to enjoy as you're setting things up!

Here's what you'll need:

→ Potato chips that are flat and even (like Pringles or Baked Lays)

→ Potato chips with ridges (like Ruffles or Wavy Lays)

→ An iron

Set it up:

1. Place the iron down on the counter and position your elf on it.

2. Group the potato chips with ridges to the left of the iron and the flat potato chips to the right.

3. Position one of the ridged potato chips under the tip of the iron so it looks like the "wrinkles" are being ironed out.

4. Depending on their awareness of what an iron is used for, this antic may not be obvious for all kids, so you may want to have your elf leave a note like, "I IRONED OUT ALL THE WRINKLES FOR YOU."

Want to make it even more fun?

Set some mini bags of the chips with ridges nearby for your child to enjoy later (or just seal up the opened bag of chips with a clip so it doesn't go stale). Since the point of this antic is the ironing, hide the flat chips and just piggy them yourself later on.

JUST THROW YOUR KID'S UNDERWEAR ON THE TREE AND CALL IT A DAY

Totally exhausted? No worries, you can still pull off an antic that will be a hilarious hit with your kids. After all, nothing is funnier than seeing underwear...anywhere!

Here's what you'll need:

→ As many clean pairs of your kid's underwear as you can sneak out of the drawer

Set it up:

1. The title says it all.

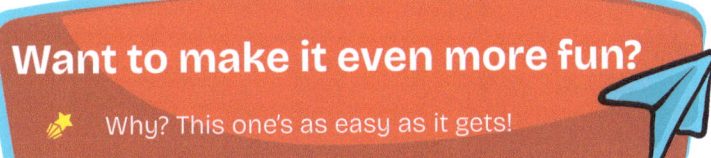

Want to make it even more fun?

✨ Why? This one's as easy as it gets!

LET'S PLAY CHESS

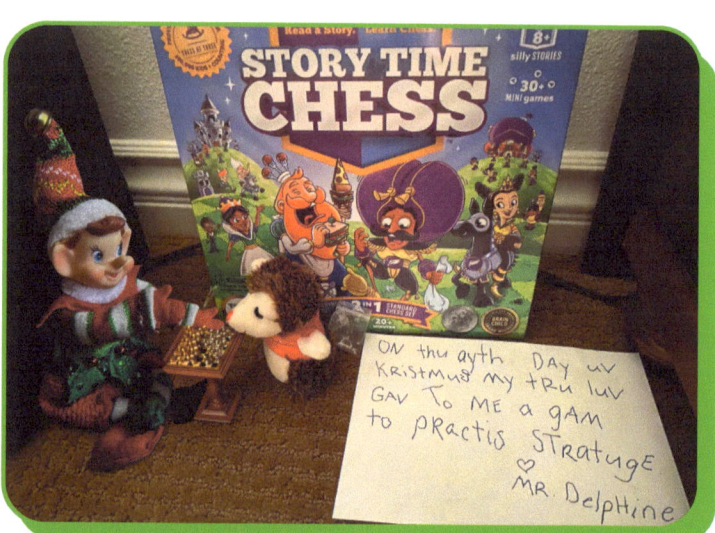

Trying to teach your little one how to play chess? This might get your kid excited to learn more about the game.

Here's what you'll need:

➜ 1 mini chess set (magnetized is best so the tiny chess pieces stay put)

➜ 1 chess tutorial game

➜ 1 miniature stuffed animal or toy figurine

Set it up:

1. This one is perfect for when you have no energy left in the tank. Simply position the mini chess set between the elf and stuffed animal and place the tutorial game nearby.

2. During this Christmas season I left a note each day with a riff on the lyrics to the 12 Days of Christmas song. For this antic, I wrote: "ON THU AYTH DAY UV KRISTMUS MY TRU LUV GAV TO ME A GAM TO PRACTIS STRATUGE."

Want to make it even more fun?

⭐ Have some other mini characters play mini checkers or mini Connect 4 nearby.

Where to Shop?

The mini chess set and the chess tutorial game can both be purchased on Amazon.

MAGIC MILK

This is a fun experiment with an immediate color burst. Do a search for Magic Milk on Pinterest, and you'll see what I'm talking about.

Here's what you'll need:

→ 1 bowl
→ Milk, preferably whole (avoid nonfat)
→ Food coloring
→ Dish Soap
→ 1 QTip

Set it up by leaving a note with these directions for your child:

1. Pour some milk in a bowl.
2. Add some drops of food coloring in the middle of the milk. Use at least 3 colors.
3. Dip a QTip in some dish soap.
4. Gently touch the surface of the milk with the QTIp and watch what happens!

Want to make it even more fun?

⭐ Provide 5 bowls of milk and experiment with different colors after completing the first one.

⭐ Extend the activity by looking up "Why does the Magic Milk experiment work" online.

MAKE ROOM FOR CANDY!

Cans of vegetables? Nah! Sacks of flour? Not needed! 50 bags of candy? Now THAT'S a pantry!

Here's what you'll need:

➜ A variety of bags/boxes of candy

Set it up:

1. Make as big of a mess with this as you have the patience to clean up (or that your kid will be able to clean up). The sky's the limit.

2. Take all the items off a few shelves of your pantry and scatter them around the house as if your elf was cleaning the pantry out and randomly discarding the unwanted items over his shoulder. Put some in piles on the kitchen counters, floor, and table. Then, take it a step further and arrange some in the hallway, dining room, stairwell...you get the idea!

3. Arrange the packages of candy on the newly cleaned shelves along with your elf and a note.

4. During this Christmas season I left a note each day with a riff on the lyrics to the 12 Days of Christmas song. For this antic, I wrote: "ON THU SICSTH DA UV KRISTMUS MI TRU LUV GAV TO ME MOR ROOM ON THU SHELFS FOR CANDE."

Want to make it even more fun?

⭐ Instead of placing the pantry items all over the place, throw them in several large trashbags and tie them up. Leave the trashbags sitting next to the pantry door or even the garage door.

⭐ Instead of candy, buy 10 or more cheap bottles of maple syrup and straws and position them as ready to drink in the pantry.

MARSHMALLOW TIC-TAC-TOE

Winner gets to eat all the marshmallows!

Here's what you'll need:

→ 9 marshmallows, all the same size

→ 1 paintbrush and edible food coloring paste (or use a marker/paint and then throw away the marshmallows later)

Set it up:

1. Paint an X or an O on 6 of the marshmallows. Leave the others plain.

2. Arrange the marshmallows in 3 rows of 3, like a Tic Tac Toe game.

3. Position your family's elf and a stuffed animal near the game, as if they're playing it.

4. Set the bag of marshmallows by the elf, along with the paintbrush.

Want to make it even more fun?

⭐ Make a game out of giant campfire-sized marshmallows for 2 large stuffed animals/toys, a game out of large marshmallows for your elf and another similar-sized toy, and a game out of mini marshmallows for 2 miniature toys.

NAUGHTY! NAUGHTY!

Drawing mustaches, horns, and beards on the family pictures? That's very naughty, but lots of fun!

Here's what you'll need:

➔ A dry erase marker
➔ A few framed pictures of your kid and/or family

Set it up:

1. Draw a mustache, beard, and/or horns on the glass of each picture.
2. Set your elf nearby, holding the dry erase marker.

Want to make it even more fun?

⭐ Have your elf make Mom into an angel.
⭐ Draw reindeer antlers instead and affix tiny red pompoms to each person's nose.
⭐ Write little sayings on the glass as well.
⭐ Do this on every glass-framed picture around the house.

NUTCRACKER STUDIO

Someone has to paint all those Nutcrackers. Might as well bring your kid into the mix!

Here's what you'll need:

→ Mini artist palate, or just use a brush and watercolor paint set you already have on hand

→ A paint-your-own nutcracker set

→ A small set of 6 nutcrackers (already painted)

Set it up:

1. Set the mini artist palate by your family's elf.

2. Position the small set of nutcrackers next to your elf, as if he just finished painting them.

3. Set the paint-your-own nutcracker nearby, adding a note, if you'd like.

Want to make it even more fun?

⭐ Instead of buying a small set of nutcrackers, gather some of the nutcrackers you already have around the house and have your family's elf draw portraits of them.

⭐ Same as above, but instead of painting portraits, paint some funny faces on some walnuts and stick them in the nutcrackers' mouths.

Where to Shop?

→ World Market sells small nutcracker sets, and you can sometimes find them at TJ Maxx and Homegoods.

→ Michael's and Hobby Lobby usually sell paint your own sets around the holidays.

O' CHIPMUS TREE

It's pretty hard to top a Christmas tree, but converting it into a Chipmus tree may be the next best thing!

Here's what you'll need:

→ About 40 snack-sized bags of assorted chips

→ About 40 sturdy clothes pins (get the kind that have a spring)

→ Whatever Christmas tree you're using this year

→ A copy of some sheet music with music notes on it – preferably notes to the song *O' Christmas Tree* (you don't need the whole song, just a couple of lines of the song are fine)

Set it up:

1. Using 1 clothes pin per chip bag, clip the various bags of chips on your Christmas tree's branches.

2. On the sheet music, write the changed lyrics to the song. I wrote it as:

   O CHIPMUS TREE
   O CHIPMUS TREE
   HOW LUVLY ARE
   THY BRANCHES!

Where to Shop?

→ It's usually a little less expensive to buy boxes with 50 bags of chips at Sam's Club, Costco, and BJs.

→ Target, Walmart, and Amazon sell clothes pins. Colored clothes pins are sold on Amazon.

Want to make it even more fun?

🎉 Change the chip bags to popcorn and the lyrics to "O Popcorn Tree".

🎉 Use a regular or jumbo-size bag of chips as the tree topper.

🎉 Open up a bag or two of chips and scatter them on the floor around the base of the tree.

ON-CALL MECHANIC

We use a lot of machinery at the North Pole, so I know my way around an engine. That's why I'm happy to provide annual tune ups during my home visits.

Here's what you'll need:

➔ 1 set of tiny tools (or use some tools you already have around the house)

➔ Several toy cars and trucks

Where to Shop?

Tiny tool kits are sold on Amazon and Etsy. The 1:12 scale is a perfect size.

Set it up:

1. Position the vehicles in a straight line, with the tallest vehicle first.

2. Place your family's elf underneath the first vehicle, with the tiny toolbox nearby.

3. Scatter a tool or two next to one of your elf's hands.

Want to make it even more fun?

⭐ Make 3 service stalls. Have two toy figurines or stuffed animals working on 2 other trucks nearby. Form 3 lines of waiting vehicles instead of just one. Larger "mechanics" can be given kid-sized tools (or they can just share the mini tool kit that the elf is using).

⭐ Use the same scenario as above but form one line of vehicles and have each toy working on something different: One changes the tires, one works underneath the car, and one washes the car.

ORANGE YOU GLAD IT'S MORNING?

Orange juice doesn't get any fresher than this!

Here's what you'll need:

➜ 1 orange
➜ 2 adhesive wiggle eyes
➜ Straw
➜ Hot glue gun & glue stick
➜ Permanent marker

Set it up:

1. Set the orange down on the counter to determine the best place to draw a face.
2. Using the marker, draw 2 eyebrows and a surprised-looking mouth.
3. Glue the eyes onto the orange.
4. Make a hole on the top of the orange and stick a straw in it.
5. Position the elf so that it looks like it's drinking from the straw.

Want to make it even more fun?

 Leave a note like "Orange you glad Christmas is almost here?"

Where to Shop?

Wiggle eyes are sold at most craft stores and by Amazon.

OUT OF THIS WORLD DELIVERY BACKUPS

Always have a backup delivery method on hand just in case Santa's sleigh breaks down.

Here's what you'll need:

- → 1 new space-related toy vehicle to give as a gift
- → Several space-related figurines from your kid's toybox

Set it up:

1. Position the various toys in an area with the following note: "If Santa's sleigh breaks down, I found some friends who will help deliver toys to good girls and boys. They're out of this world!"

Want to make it even more fun?

⭐ Add some wrapped mini presents to each vehicle.

Where to Shop?

This antic was inspired when I found this light up, spinning UFO in the toy section at Walgreens.

THE PERFECT HIDING SPOT

They'll never guess where I'm hiding!

Here's what you'll need:

→ 1 new box of tissue

Set it up:

1. Pull all of the tissue out of the box.

2. Scatter all but one sheet of tissue on the floor and on the furniture around the box, as if your family's elf was tossing the sheets over his shoulder in his hurry to find a hiding spot.

3. Position the elf with his legs inside the hole in the box but his arms, chest, and head peeking out.

4. Place the one sheet of tissue on top of the elf's head, as if he's trying to hide himself. Make sure it sticks up like a big bump.

5. Place a note on the floor just outside your child's bedroom door saying, "Bet you can't find me!"

Want to make it even more fun?

⭐ Open up several cupboards, drawers, and closets and make a bit of a mess, as if the elf was trying to find some good hiding spots.

PERFECTLY PHYSICS

Use an antic to teach a little science. Here, Newton's principles are on full display when simply using a common desk decoration.

Here's what you'll need:

➜ 1 Newton's Cradle (see the picture)

➜ 2 toy figurines

Set it up:

1. Place the Newton's Cradle on a flat surface with the 2 figurines on either side.

2. Write a note to have the 2 figures battle it out. Best 2 out of 3 games wins. During this Christmas season I left a note each day with a riff on the lyrics to the 12 Days of Christmas song. For this antic, I wrote: "ON THU TWELF DAY UV KRISTMUS MY TRU LUV GAVE TO ME PEEZUH AND TAWCO CONTEST BEST 2 OUT UV 3!"

3. Your child will soon get a mini-lesson in physics and realize that there is no true winner, given the conservation of momentum with this device!

Want to make it even more fun?

⭐ Desktop Newton's Cradles are often sold in the holiday gift section of CVS and Walgreens for less than $10. They're also available on Amazon.

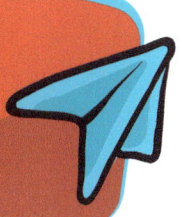

PICELFSO

Most elves have quite a unique artistic side, but not everyone appreciates their work. I guess that's because art is so subjective.

Here's what you'll need:

→ A mini chalkboard easel with chalk or a mini painting easel with a mini canvas and brush

→ Paper, paint, and/or colored pencils

Set it up:

1. Draw a rudimentary picture of a reindeer from the perspective of standing behind it and then color or paint it. I labeled my picture as "SANTA'S VIEW FRUM HIS SLEY RAINDEER BUTT."

2. Draw another rudimentary picture of Santa with a pig's face and then color or paint it.

3. Post the pictures somewhere and then set your elf on a nearby table or stand.

4. Draw an angel on the chalkboard and label it with your child's name. Place the easel and your elf's art supplies near him on the stand.

Want to make it even more fun?

⭐ Have your elf draw/paint funny individual portraits of each family member.

Where to Shop?

→ This mini easel was purchased in the toy section at Target.

→ Mini chalkboard easels can also often be found at Micheal's, Hobby Lobby, and on Amazon. Keep an eye when stores are stocking back to school items in dollar bins.

POPCORN PALOOZA

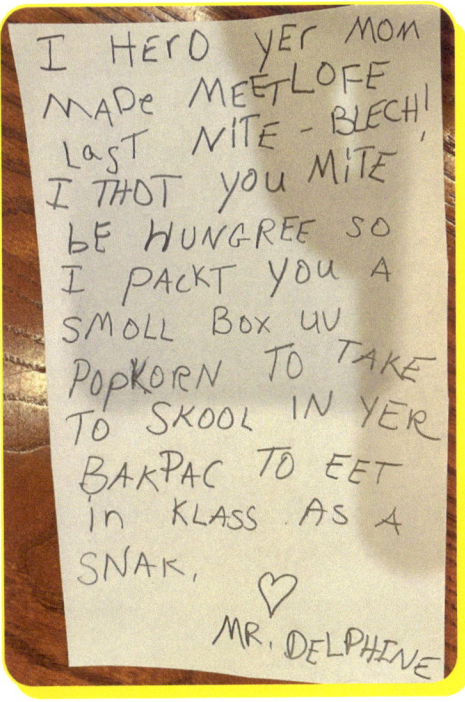

I HErO yEr MoM MAD̄e MEETLOFE LAST NITE - BLECH! I THOT yOu MITE bE HUNGREE SO I PACKT yOu A SMOLL BOX uv POPKORN TO TAKE TO SKOOL IN YER BAKPAC TO EET iN KLASS AS A SNAK,

♡

MR. DELPHINE

Sometimes elves aren't the best at understanding portion control. But hey, who doesn't mind a little extra popcorn?!?

Here's what you'll need:

→ 20+ bags of microwave popcorn

→ As many toy dump trucks (or other toy vehicles that can transport some popcorn) you can round up

→ Toy shovel or large scoop

→ A big box (shipping size is great)

→ A tall, thin box to use as a popcorn chute for the dump trucks to unload their popcorn into the main box

Set it up:

1. First, a word of caution: Do **NOT** microwave each bag of popcorn one after the other because you'll probably break the microwave, like I did (really!). Instead, spread out the microwaving over several days and just store the bags in a hiding spot.

2. Decide on how you want to stage the box and the trucks to make it look like an assembly line from the microwave to the big popcorn box.

3. I decided to use the landing on our stairs for the main box of popcorn. Then, I positioned the dump trucks so they were driving in a line from the microwave to the half-wall of the stairway. I leaned a long, narrow box against the wall so the dump trucks could "drive" up the box to dump their loads into the box that sat below on the landing.

4. Crumple up some of the popcorn bags and throw them on the floor. While you're making a mess, you might as well scatter some popcorn around as well.

5. Position your elf on the kitchen counter with an open bag of popcorn nearby. Place a toy shovel or large scoop in the bag.

6. Leave a note. Mine said: "I HERD YER MOM MADE MEETLOFF LAST NITE – BLECH! I THOT YOU MITE BE HUNGREE SO I PACKT YOU A SMOLL BOX UV POPKORN TO TAKE TO SKOOL IN YER BAKPAC TO EET IN KLASS AS A SNAK."

Want to make it even more fun?

⭐ You could build a connecting PVC pipe system (or other expandable tube system) that leads from the microwave area to where the box will be – it doesn't have to be in the next room.

⭐ Place popcorn in shoeboxes that are connected to and being pulled by toy cars, plastic horses, or stuffed animals to the final big box.

⭐ Fill up a big trash bag with popcorn and tie a string that connects it to the back of your child's bike seat.

Where to Shop?

→ It may be cheaper to buy popcorn bags from Sam's Club, Costco, or BJs for this antic.

→ All of the big plastic dump trucks pictured here were purchased over several years at Target.

POTTY SONGS

Everyone likes party...oh, I mean potty, songs. Just write the song titles on some rolls of toilet paper, and you'll have a great songfest ready to go!

Here's what you'll need:

→ 7 rolls of toilet paper
→ Fine-tipped markers of different colors

Set it up:

1. Write one of the following song titles or sayings on a square of each roll of toilet paper, along with some artistic touches:

   - Have Yourself a Potty Little Christmas
   - All I Want for Christmas Is POO
   - We Wish You a Stinky Christmas
   - Rockin' Around the Christmas Pee
   - Jingle Bells, Your Poop Smells
   - It's the Most Stinkiest Time of the Year
   - Last Christmas, I Gave You My Fart

2. Stack the toilet paper rolls on top of the toilet so they're ready for a go!

Want to make it even more fun?

Looking for other song titles? Try these:

⭐ Deck the Halls with Fecal Matter
⭐ Silent Fart, Stinky Room
⭐ Frosty the Poopman
⭐ O Come, All Ye Farting

RAIN CLOUD

Little ones will love to watch the wonder of making colorful "rain".

Here's what you'll need:

- → A clear glass
- → A can of shaving cream
- → Food coloring

Set it up:

1. Set the glass, shaving cream, and food coloring bottles on the table.
2. Write a note with these directions: "Let's make a magic cloud! Fill the glass with water. Spray a cloud of shaving cream on top. Squeeze a few drops of food coloring on top of the cloud and watch it rain!"

Want to make it even more fun?

⭐ Turn this into a learning experience. Experiment with primary colors (red, blue, yellow) to try to make orange, purple, green, and turquoise rain.

RAINBOW MAKER

Bring a little color into your morning with this sweet activity.

Here's what you'll need:

➜ 2 packages of Skittles (or 1 king sized bag – you'll need about 40, depending on the diameter of the plate you're using)

➜ 1 dinner plate

➜ Hot water

➜ A note with this message: "LET'S MAKE A RAINBOW! HAVE YOUR MOM POUR SOME HOT WATER ON THE PLATE AND WATCH WHAT HAPPENS!"

Set it up:

1. Separate the colors of the Skittles.
2. Position the candies in this order around the edge of the sunken part of the plate: 2 purple, 2 green, 2 yellow, 2 orange, 2 red. Repeat this pattern until you have a full circle.
3. Once your kid is up, boil some water.
4. Gently pour the water into the center of the plate until the water reaches the Skittles and then sit back and be amazed!

Want to make it even more fun?

⭐ Leave an extra bag of Skittles as a gift, since your kid won't be able to eat the ones on the plate.

⭐ Buy a family-sized bag of Skittles and redo this with different alternating colors to see what the most impressive patterns are.

REINDEER LESSONS

Looking to switch jobs? Why not train to be a reindeer? Join us in this informative training session!

Here's what you'll need:

→ 30 brown pipe cleaners

→ 15 very small red pom poms (about the size of a pea)

→ 2 books about Rudolph or Santa's reindeer

→ White paper and fine tipped markers or colored pencils to make a few mini posters

→ 14 animal figurines

→ Glue gun & glue sticks or another tacky substance to attach the pom poms to the animals

Set it up:

1. Create 15 sets of antlers out of the pipe cleaners and wrap them around each toy animal's head. Wrap the last set around the elf's head.

2. Attach the pom poms to each animal's nose. If using a glue gun will disfigure the animals, use another sticky substance.

3. Create some teaching posters for your elf to refer to. I like to include a syllabus and a diagram.

4. Position the animals as if they're in a classroom being taught by the elf.

Where to Shop?

I couldn't find packages of brown pipe cleaners at any of the stores near me, so I purchased them on Amazon, along with the pom poms.

Want to make it even more fun?

Get creative with the topics:

✦ The Basics of Becoming a Flying Furball

✦ Mastering the Art of Prancing

✦ Creating the Perfect Jingle Sound

✦ Tricks to Impress Santa and the Elves

✦ The Importance of Napping Between Flights

REINDEER TRAINING ACADEMY

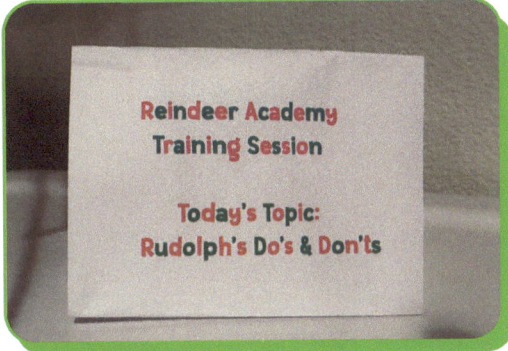

Reindeer Academy
Training Session

Today's Topic:
Rudolph's Do's & Don'ts

At the North Pole, we take safety seriously. Just like airline pilots, our reindeer take continuing education classes to retain their flying certification. You can host one of those classes in your home.

Here's what you'll need:

➔ Several reindeer – they don't all need to be the same kind

➔ A toy movie projector or a tv screen

➔ A "Reindeer Training Academy" sign with today's training topic

Set it up:

1. Set up the "screen" area. If you're using an old-time film projector, like the one pictured here, position it so the movie "projects" onto something. I used a chalkboard easel like we're back in 1978, but you can also just use the wall.

2. No need to go out and purchase a projector for this activity. You can just as easily position the reindeer in front of a tv or tablet that's playing a flight school simulator video on YouTube.

3. Make it look like a classroom by positioning the reindeer in rows.

4. Create a sign to place by the screen with the title of the training and today's topic.

Want to make it even more fun?

Get creative with the topics:

- 🌠 **Advanced Sleigh Navigation: No GPS Required!** Find the best shortcuts through blizzards and avoid awkward encounters with confused penguins.

- 🌠 **Flying 101: How to Prevent Mid-Air Antlers Tangling** Important techniques to avoid collision and maintain personal space in the air, including demonstrations with inflatable antler suits.

- 🌠 **Prancing for Dummies: Fancier Hoofwork that Dazzles** A fun ballet class to help reindeer master their graceful movements, complete with tutus.

Where to Shop?

- → The 5 bean bag reindeer in this picture were purchased at the Bullseye's Playground & Dollar Spot at Target for five bucks. This area typically carries inexpensive figurines around the holidays, as do dollar stores.

- → The film projector is an animated Peanuts holiday figurine that was purchased in the holiday section at CVS.

REMOTE CONTROLLED FUN

Elves love playing with remote controlled vehicles too!

Here's what you'll need:

→ A remote-controlled vehicle
→ Other similar-type vehicles

Set it up:

1. Option 1 (pictured): Group 3 or 4 similar types of vehicles around the remote-controlled device, as if they're on a mission or completing a job. Position the remote device on the elf.

2. Option 2: Set up a car race from one end of the room to the other, complete with a start and finish sign. Place the cars in different position in the race, with the remote-controlled vehicle in the lead. Position the elf so he's controlling the remote device. Set up stuffed animals and toy figurines on the sidelines, cheering the race drivers on.

Want to make it even more fun?

⭐ Turn 3 bottles of sprinkles on their sides, stacking 1 bottle on top of the other 2 like they're logs. Use thin gift wrap ribbon or string to attach the bottles to the remote-controlled device. Set the elf in one room with the device and the vehicle with the sprinkles in another room, as if it's delivering the sprinkles to the elf.

⭐ Same idea as above, but attach a scoop or measuring cup with dry pet food. Place the bag of dry pet food by the elf. Instead of having the vehicle driving towards the elf, have the vehicle approaching the pet's food bowl.

RETRIBUTION

Has your kid been annoying you lately? Annoy them back!

Here's what you'll need:

- → 100 red plastic cups (or any color, as long as they're not clear)
- → 100 pennies
- → Hot glue gun and glue sticks
- → A note saying "(Your kid's name), I hid $1.00 in these cups. Find it!"

Set it up:

1. Warm up your glue gun, using the lowest setting possible so it doesn't burn through the plastic cup.
2. Glue 1 penny on the bottom inside of each cup.
3. Place the cups upside down all over the floor of the room.
4. Leave the note on the floor just outside your kid's room.

Want to make it even more fun?

⭐ If you really want your kid to work for the money, glue quarters instead of pennies (and change the note to $25) so that he/she is more motivated to peel off each coin.

ROASTED ELF

It's all fun and games until you happen to step into the wrong territory. Then you can really get yourself in a pickle, as I did here!

Here's what you'll need:

→ Bamboo skewers or sticks

→ Hot glue gun & glue sticks

→ Twine

→ Miniature campfire figurine (preferably one that lights up)

→ A bottle of ketchup, A1 or BBQ sauce

→ A fork

→ A toy figurine or stuffed animal that may be viewed as a little villainous

Set it up:

1. Glue the bamboo skewers together to resemble something that looks like a roasting spit. Make sure it's wide enough to hang your elf on it.
2. Tie your elf's hands and legs to the top of the spit so that his back will be against the fire.
3. Position the campfire near an outlet (if needed) and place the pit with the elf over it.
4. Scatter plastic jewels, wood chips, or shredded paper Easter basket grass around the campfire, if desired.
5. Place the "villain" toy next to the bottle of ketchup and fork, supervising the roasting.

Want to make it even more fun?

⭐ Place a pile of mini skeleton bones nearby.

⭐ Position a group of "running" army men or stuffed animals that are charging in to save the day.

Where to Shop?

Any kind of shop that sells holiday village figurines is your best bet to find a campfire that lights up. I found this one at a Hallmark store.

ROCKIN' AROUND THE CACTUS TREE

I like to gather up a few friends and put on a performance around the Christmas tree for all to enjoy. Just don't get too close to this tree or you might get pricked!

Here's what you'll need:

➜ Animated Christmas Cactus that plays music and dances

➜ Miniature instruments

➜ Various figurines to play the musicians and the audience

Set it up:

1. Place the cactus in the "orchestra area" and set your elf and an instrument next to it.

2. Arrange some of the figurines and their instruments in the orchestra area.

3. Position the remainder of the figurines as audience members facing the musicians.

Want to make it even more fun?

⭐ Have your elf provide clues as to where to find each musician around the house and then gather them all together for a performance.

⭐ Buy a real instrument that your child shows interest in playing and set it nearby with a placeholder sign with his/her name on it.

⭐ Instead of buying mini instruments, draw some for the musicians on cardstock.

⭐ B. Toys sells a B. Symphony Musical Toy Orchestra that's a big hit with kids because it can play 6 instruments at a time, so they can create hundreds of different songs. Your toy figurines could use the instruments that come with this set instead of the miniature ones that don't play anything.

Where to Shop?

➜ CVS and Walgreens often sell animatronic holiday figures in their seasonal aisle.

➜ The B. Symphony Musical Toy Orchestra can currently be purchased online through Walmart and Amazon.

SACK RACES

First one to the finish line gets to drink all the syrup in the house!

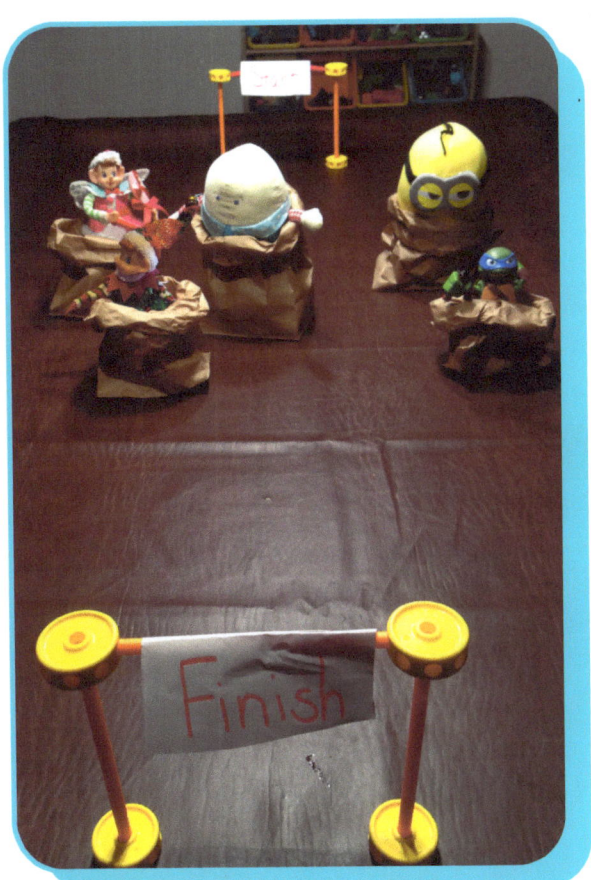

Here's what you'll need:

→ About 4 brown paper lunch bags
→ A variety of action figures and stuffed animals
→ "Start" and "Finish" signs

Set it up:

1. Station the start and finish signs on a table.
2. Roll each of the bags down a bit to simulate a sack and place a figurine inside.
3. Position the figurines on the table as if they're racing each other to the finish line.

Want to make it even more fun?

 Position a variety of figurines on either side of the sack race as if the crowd is cheering them on.

SCAVENGER HUNT #1: SEEK AND FIND

Instead of hide and seek, play seek and find!

Here's what you'll need:

→ A scavenger hunt list (just make sure that you have all the items listed).

→ Note from your elf that says: "Let's go on a scavenger hunt! See if you can find all 10 of these items." Then list the items your kid should find.

→ Suggestions

- 1 candy cane
- A roll of gift wrap that has Santa on it
- 2 cookie cutters
- A red and a green crayon
- Something round
- The same number of squares of toilet paper as there are days until Christmas
- A selfie of your toes by the Christmas tree
- A green toy
- 5 Q Tips
- A coin that's dated before 2007

Set it up:

1. Position your elf in a room with the note and watch the chaos ensue.

Want to make it even more fun?

⭐ Offer a prize if all items are brought back in a certain amount of time.

⭐ For older kids, really put the pressure on. If they can bring back all of the items to the elf in 3 minutes (or what's stressful but doable), they'll get a large prize. If they don't but can bring it back in the next 2 or 3 minutes, they'll get a medium prize. If they don't but bring it all back, they'll get a consolation prize. Just be careful with this – you don't want any hurt feelings!

SCAVENGER HUNT #2: RIDDLE ME THIS

You'll have to solve each riddle to reach the main prize!

Christmas colors are green and red.

The next clue will be where you rest your head.

Here's what you'll need:

→ A set of Scavenger Hunt riddle cards where the reader has to solve the riddle on one card to find the next clue. These are available for free on many online sites, so all you have to do is write each riddle on a different card. Or, if you want to save a little time or effort, Etsy sells pre-designed cards. Just print them out and cut them apart. Google "Christmas scavenger hunt clues" to see the available options.

→ A prize to find with the last card

Set it up:

1. Leave the first riddle card in your elf's lap. Then place the remaining cards around the house where each preceding card directs the reader to go.

2. Hide the prize in the location where the last card sends the reader.

Want to make it even more fun?

✨ Tape a mini candy cane or Hershey's kiss to each card.

SHOESHINE

It's important to always present your best self from head to toe. I'm a master shoe shiner!

Here's what you'll need:

- ➔ Aluminum foil
- ➔ 2 or 3 pairs of your kid's shoes
- ➔ Paper and pen for a note

Set it up:

1. Wrap each shoe completely in aluminum foil, shiniest side up.
2. Write a note so that your kid understands the joke. Here's the note I left: "TIS THE SEASON TO SPARKLE, SO I GAVE YOU A SHOESHINE!"

Want to make it even more fun?

- ⭐ Wrap up flip flops as well.
- ⭐ Have your family's elf shine the whole family's shoes.

SILLY STRING BATTLE

It's a battle to the end . . . of the silly string can!

Here's what you'll need:

→ 2 cans of silly string
→ Several blocks or toy building materials to make 2 barriers
→ A group of toy figurines
→ Optional: Military boats, tanks, and/or trucks

Where to Shop?

Silly string can often be found at dollar stores, Walmart, and Target.

Set it up:

1. Build 2 barriers that sit a couple of feet away from each other on a counter or table.
2. Set the action figures behind one of the barriers in various fighting positions.
3. Note: You probably won't want to spray your family's elf with silly string because its chemicals may discolor his face/clothing. Spray only the items that you're not concerned about getting discolored.
4. Before setting your elf in position, spray both barrier sides with silly string, making sure some lands in between the barriers as well.
5. Position 1 can of silly string on each side, facing the "enemy side."
6. Position your elf.
7. Close the door to the room so your pets don't try to eat the silly string.

Want to make it even more fun?

⭐ Position some military vehicles (e.g., boats, tanks, trucks) just outside of the room, facing the closed door, as if ready to enter and attack.

⭐ Set up this scene in a bathtub/shower area and spray the silly string all over the shower walls, making sure that some hangs off the shower rod and the faucet spout.

SINGING FOR SANTA

What's Christmas without a little caroling? And there's nothing better than singing for Santa!

Here's what you'll need:

- → About 15 empty soda cans (preferably from the same soda brand)
- → Adhesive wiggle eyes (at least 30 medium-sized)
- → Hot glue gun & glue sticks
- → Santa figurine
- → Another figurine to use as the "choir director"

Set it up:

1. Rinse out the cans and dry them so you don't have ants joining the performance.

2. Remove the tabs from each can and discard.

3. The opening of the can will act as the mouth. The dot that's leftover after the tabs are removed will serve as the nose.

4. Hold the can with both hands, joining your thumbs at the middle of the can under where the opening is. Scrunch the cans just slightly in the middle so they all bend over just a bit (see picture). Don't squeeze too much – you want the cans to all be about the same height and still sit upright.

5. Using the hot glue gun, glue 2 wiggle eyes just above the dot that was left after the can's tab was removed.

6. Position the cans in a choir-like setup near Santa, with your family's elf nearby, and then set the choir director in front of the cans.

Where to Shop?

Wiggle eyes can be purchased at Hobby Lobby and most craft stores.

Want to make it even more fun?

- ⭐ Play Christmas music sung by a choir.
- ⭐ Include a larger audience of toys.
- ⭐ Have the cans "hold" mini books of sheet music.

SIPPY STRAW

It's time to construct the world's longest straw and see if it works!

Here's what you'll need:

→ 1 package of flexible plastic straws
→ 1 bottle of syrup

Set it up:

1. Position your family's elf on top of a cabinet.
2. Set the bottle of syrup on a countertop below.
3. Connect the straws together by flattening one end of the straw and inserting it into another straw. You may want to secure the connections with clear tape.
4. Place one end of the straw near the elf's mouth and place the other end in the bottle of maple syrup.

Want to make it even more fun?

⭐ Make 3 or 4 drinks instead of just one using chocolate syrup, corn syrup, and a bottle of soda. Place the other bottles on different counters and then tie the 4 straws together at the top by the elf's mouth.

SNOWBALL CATAPULT FIGHT

This antic originated when my family's kid made a rover device out of his connector toys. His mom thought it looked just like a snowball launcher, so I took off with the idea. Now that was one powerful snowball fight advantage!

Here's what you'll need:

→ 20+ white pom poms at least 2" in diameter (cotton balls or large marshmallows will also work)

→ A catapult-type device (make your own or buy a catapult kit)

→ Figurines (toy or Christmas-themed)

Where to Shop?

→ These "snowballs" were purchased as a holiday kit at Target.

→ Craft stores sell giant pom poms.

→ These connector toys are sold online as STEM engineering building blocks.

Set it up:

1. Position your family's elf with the catapult on one side of an area and a group of toys on the other.

2. If you'd like, construct 2 walls for each side out of large marshmallows or blocks for the figures to stand behind.

3. Stack some of the pom pom "snowballs" next to each side.

4. Knock a few of the toys down as if they were hit by the flying "snowballs".

Want to make it even more fun?

⭐ Have a slingshot snowball fight instead.

⭐ If you can get your hands on a snowcone machine, your elf could host a snowcone party after the snowball fight.

SNOWFLAKES

Santa says every snowflake is unique, just like us elves!

Here's what you'll need:

→ 1 package of Q Tips (the number you'll need will depend on the size and number of snowflakes being made)

Set it up:

1. Make a snowflake pattern on the floor with the Q Tips.

Want to make it even more fun?

⭐ Place the box nearby, with a bottle of glue, for your kid to make his own snowflake patterns to hang.

STICKY WIPE

Substituting a roll of duct tape for a roll of toilet paper could create a very sticky situation!

Here's what you'll need:

→ A roll of duct tape or masking tape
→ A Sharpie marker

Set it up:

1. About 4 inches from where the tape ends, write "Talk about a sticky situation!" or "This could get a little sticky!" on the tape.
2. Place the roll of tape on the toilet paper holder.
3. Unroll about 6 inches of the tape so the message hangs down like toilet paper. You may want to crease the end of the tape into a triangle like hotels do with toilet paper.
4. Position your family's elf, with the marker, nearby.

Want to make it even more fun?

🌠 Substitute the rolls of toilet paper in all of the bathrooms in the house with rolls of tape and then add in a mission where your kid has to find where your elf hid all the toilet paper rolls.

STOCKINGS FILLED WITH... UNDERWEAR?!?

Underwear is just one of those things that is funny no matter where you see it!

Here's what you'll need:

→ Several pairs of your kid's underwear

→ Christmas stockings

→ Optional: Additional gifts from your family's elf

Set it up:

1. Stuff underwear in the stockings and rehang them. Make sure some pairs of underwear are sticking out of the top.

2. Throw a few pairs of underwear on a nearby Christmas tree or holiday decoration as well.

3. Since this was Christmas Eve and my last visit for the year, I added in a few sweet parting gifts as well.

Want to make it even more fun?

⭐ Leave a trail of toilet paper that leads from your kid's bedroom to the stockings.

⭐ Stuff Mom's stocking with her underwear and Dad's with his.

⭐ Hide the stockings with a note directing your kid to hunt for the stockings that have been filled with a special surprise.

Where to Shop?

The Elf Pizza Kit and mini gingerbread house pictured here were purchased on Etsy.

STORAGE ROOM SHOOT OUT

There's a new gang in town with its eyes on some prime territory in the storage room closet!

Here's what you'll need:

- → 15 to 20 stuffed animals and/or toy figurines of different sizes
- → Nerf guns
- → A mini water gun or Nerf gun for your elf
- → Nerf bullets

Set it up:

1. Stage the toys on two different sides of the closet/room looking at each other.
2. Position some Nerf guns by them.
3. Scatter the bullets around the area.

Want to make it even more fun?

- ★ Increase the scale and take up the entire room/hallway that's right outside your kid's bedroom door, scattering Nerf bullets all over the floor.
- ★ Make the battle appear like it's over who can use the bathroom next.

Where to Shop?

Cracker Barrel and Amazon often sell the "World's Smallest" toys – which are miniature versions of well-loved toys.

STORY TIME FOR TOYS

With all the excitement, sometimes it's nice to just sit back and relax with a good book. Gather up the toys for story time!

Here's what you'll need:

→ A Christmas book

→ A collection of toy figurines, trains, or stuffed animals

Set it up:

1. Open up the book and position your family's elf next to it, as if he's reading to the toys.
2. Position the toys around the book.

Want to make it even more fun?

⭐ Give each toy its own mini book to read.

⭐ Place a small, gift-wrapped basket of Christmas books for your child next to the elf.

⭐ Put a pair of reading glasses on your elf.

STUCK IN THE CLAW MACHINE

When I was loading up this claw machine with toys, I didn't realize I'd get stuck. A little help here, please?!?

Here's what you'll need:

→ 1 claw machine filled with mini toys (this is a GREAT gift for kids 5-8)

→ A figurine to play the machine

Where to Shop?
Amazon sells a variety of claw machines and packages of mini toys.

Set it up:

1. My family's kid says that this claw machine is one of the top 5 gifts he's ever received (even after 10 years). So, while it's pricey for an elf's antic, it's been included in this book because many people don't realize you can purchase them.

2. Dump the toys in the claw machine and set your family's elf inside, making sure he's looking out.

3. Position another toy outside, so that it's working the controller.

Want to make it even more fun?

⭐ Stick a few dollar bills or candy bars in the mix.

⭐ Fill the claw machine with aliens and Woody, like in Toy Story.

⭐ For a funny gift, fill it with travel-sized tubes of toothpaste and mini toothbrushes.

TASTE TEST

Ever bite into a delicious-looking apple only to find that it's mealy and tastes horrible? Let me do the work and find the perfect apple for your next snack!

Here's what you'll need:

→ About a dozen cheap apples (or ones that you can bake in a treat a little later in the day)

Set it up:

1. Wash the apples and take a small bite out of each one.
2. Place all but one of the apples in a fruit bowl on the counter.
3. Set the remaining apple next to the elf, along with a note like "(Insert kid's name), I TAYST TESTED ALL THU APPULS TO FIND YOU THU BEST WUN FER YOUR LUNCH. HERE'S THE WINNER. NJOY!"

Want to make it even more fun?

⭐ Use a combination of different fruits. Cut 1 slice from an orange or mango, peel off just one section of skin on all the bananas (leaving them hanging on the banana holder, if you use one), take a bite out of a few strawberries, and then place the winning fruit by your elf.

TOILET BOWL TOOTHBRUSH

Using a toilet brush to clean your teeth may leave them stinkier than when you started.

Here's what you'll need:

→ 1 toilet brush – the grungier, the better

→ Toothpaste (brightly colored works better for this antic than white)

Set it up:

1. Place the toilet bowl brush in the bathroom sink.

2. Set your elf nearby the handle.

3. Squeeze toothpaste all over the brush, as well as around the sink.

4. During this Christmas season I left a note each day with a riff on the lyrics to the 12 Days of Christmas song. For this antic, I wrote: "ON THU SEVENTH DA UV KRISTMUS MI TRU LUV GAV TO ME SUMTHING TO BRUSH MI TEETH."

5. Leave a note so your kid understands the joke. I left a second note with: "(Insert kid's name) <u>DON'T</u> USE THIS BRUSH! IT LEFT MI BRETH EVEN STEENKEER THAN BEFOR I USED IT. NOW MI BRETH SMELS LIK FARTS!!!"

Want to make it even more fun?

🌟 Have your elf "gift" your child a brand-new toilet bowl brush as a toothbrush.

🌟 Make even more of a mess with the toothpaste – spread it on the mirror, the floor, and around the bowl of the toilet.

🌟 Have your elf confuse the toilet bowl for a sink so that he's brushing his teeth using the water of the toilet bowl.

TP PATROL

There's nothing like having a little toilet paper around when you need it.

Here's what you'll need:

→ 1 mega sized roll of toilet paper (or a few regular size ones)

→ 1 toy truck or car big enough for your family's elf to sit in

Set it up:

1. Start unrolling the toilet paper in one room of the house and walk with it throughout the rooms in a pattern the elf might drive in.

2. When you've unwrapped all but 5 or 6 squares, place the roll in the back of the truck.

3. Position your elf as the driver of the truck.

4. During this Christmas season I left a note each day with a riff on the lyrics to the 12 Days of Christmas song. For this antic, I wrote: "ON THU SEKUND DAY OF KRISTMUS MY TRU LUV GAV TO ME SUM TP TO WIPE MY TUSHEE!"

Want to make it even more fun?

 Use more rolls of toilet paper to make it look like your elf drove in every corner of the house.

TP'D TREE

I have the perfect garland to wrap around your Christmas tree!

Here's what you'll need:

➜ A couple mega size rolls of toilet paper

Set it up:

1. You'll want to have a partner to help you with this activity so you don't have to walk around your Christmas tree a bazillion times.

2. Starting at the top of the tree, wrap the toilet paper around the width of the tree, gradually working your way down so that toilet paper pretty much covers the majority tree.

3. Leave some toilet paper on the roll and trail it to a nearby sofa or chair.

4. Stick your family's elf into the roll.

5. If you want, write how many days are left until Christmas on one of the last remaining squares.

Want to make it even more fun?

⭐ Alternate rows of toilet paper with sparkly tree garland

⭐ For an even bigger mess, also TP the entire room

⭐ Write a little jingle substituting "TP'd tree" for "Christmas tree".

UNDERWEAR HANG GLIDING

Soarin' high above the ground!

Here's what you'll need:

→ 4 pairs of your kid's underwear

→ A ceiling fan

→ Painter's tape

Set it up:

1. Position one pair of underwear on each of the ceiling fan's blades about a foot away from the motor.

2. Slide your family's elf in between the underwear and the bottom of the fan blade that faces the floor. Position the elf's arms out to make it look like he's flying.

3. If the underwear or the elf won't stay positioned when the fan is turned on, use some painter's tape to secure it.

4. Turn the fan on low right before your child wakes up.

Want to make it even more fun?

✦ Place a stuffed animal or figurine in the other pairs of underwear.

✦ Make it a party by placing 2 pairs of underwear and 2 toys on each fan blade. Just be careful to watch the weight of the objects and ensure they don't get too close to the fan's motor.

VERTICAL BLINDS

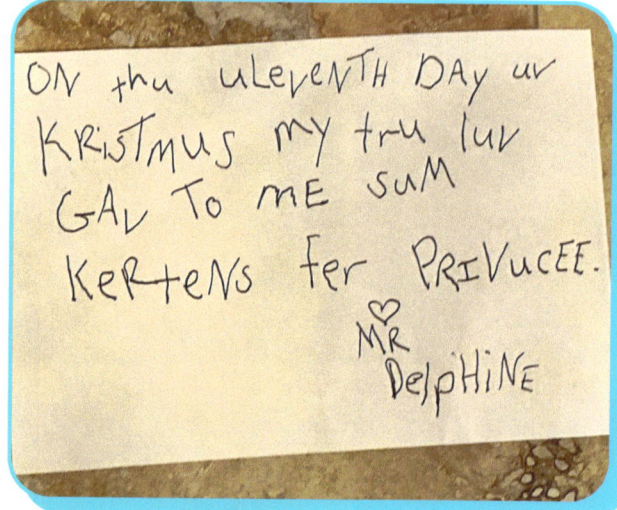

Sometimes a little privacy is needed. When you don't have drapes, you can always make your own vertical blinds or curtains out of toilet paper like I did.

Here's what you'll need:

→ About 2 mega rolls of toilet paper (or 6 typical size ones) that has a denser composite, like Charmin or Northern

→ Command Hooks and fishing line or twine if you don't have a curtain rod or garland to hang the toilet paper from

Want to make it even more fun?

⭐ Write potty-themed Christmas song lyrics on the toilet paper.

⭐ Add some silly string to make an even bigger mess.

Set it up:

1. Don't use 1-ply toilet paper sheets for this activity because it will tear too easily.

2. Choose a window or sliding glass door. If it doesn't have a curtain rod above it, position some Command Hooks and then string some fishing line or twine to make a temporary "rod" to hang the toilet paper on.

3. Hang the toilet paper in continuous sheets from the rod to the floor to mimic vertical blinds. If you have animals in the house, don't let the toilet paper touch the floor because they may walk on it, causing it to tear off.

4. When the roll has only about 15 more squares on it, place your elf inside the roll and let it dangle from the rod.

5. During this Christmas season I left a note each day with a riff on the lyrics to the 12 Days of Christmas song. For this antic, I wrote: "ON THU ULEVENTH DAY UV KRISTMUS MY TRU LUV GAV TO ME SUM KERTENS FER PRIVUCEE."

VITAMINS HELP CANDY CANES GROW

Do vitamins really help you grow big and strong? Well, just look what happened overnight with these!

Here's what you'll need:

→   A container of your kids' vitamins
→   2 sizes of candy canes (about 5 large and 5 small)
→   Houseplant in a pot

Where to Shop?

Walmart and Target often sell different sized candy canes and other types of candy in their holiday aisles.

Set it up:

1. Give your kids a box of the smaller candy canes the day before this antic to hang on the tree. They can eat a few, but just make sure there are 5 or 6 left. Or, if your kids already have a stash of candy canes in the pantry, no need to buy any more.
2. Take the larger candy canes and "plant" them in one of the houseplant pots.
3. Empty the vitamins from the container and stash them in a sealed bag in the pantry so they don't go to waste.
4. Tip the empty vitamin bottle nearby as if your family's elf planted the candy canes with the vitamins.
5. Leave a note. Mine said: "YER KANDEE KANES LOOKD PUNEE SO I GAVE THEM SUM VITUMINZ TO HELP THEM GRO."

Want to make it even more fun?

⭐ For younger kids, make this a 2-day antic. On Day 1, have your family elf gift your child a box of the smaller candy canes, along with a note with directions to plant 6 candy canes with 1 vitamin each in one of the plant pots around the house. That night, or on Day 2, replace the smaller candy canes with the larger ones before your child wakes up, discarding the vitamins.

⭐ It's not unusual around Christmas to see stores sell gigantic versions of some favorite candy bars, like Snickers and Hershey Kisses, so it's easy to substitute another type of candy for the candy canes.

VROOM VROOM SNOWMAN

Here's an indoor snowman that won't melt.

Here's what you'll need:

➔ About 50 matchbox-sized cars or mini toy figurines

Set it up:

1. Position the cars into an outline of a snowman shape by making 3 circles and a hat on top.

Want to make it even more fun?

⭐ Cut out some colored paper to make eyes, a nose, a mouth, and buttons. Use 2 sticks for arms.

⭐ Popcorn or Doritos could also be used instead of cars (as long as your pets can't get to it).

WASHING DAY

Elves are ingenious and efficient. For example, why use a washing machine AND a dryer when you can use just one machine to wash and dry underwear? Load up the dishwasher!

Here's what you'll need:

→ A pile of your kid's clean underwear

→ A dishwasher

→ Paper and marker for a note

Set it up:

1. Arrange your kid's underwear on the dishwasher racks.

2. Place the dishwashing detergent box on the countertop above the dishwasher, along with your family's elf.

3. Little ones may not get the joke, so write a note. Here's the one I wrote: "I washed your underwear for you."

Want to make it even more fun?

 Wrap the clean underwear around some dishes on the rack.

WHAT A BOWTIFUL SMILE!

Little ones won't stop smiling when they see what their family's elf has been up to!

Here's what you'll need:

→ 3 regular-sized gift bows (2 of one color and 1 of a different color)

→ 6 smaller-sized bows (all the same color)

Set it up:

1. On a mirror, affix 2 large gift bows as the eyes.

2. Position 1 gift bow underneath the eyes where the nose should go.

3. Position 6 smaller gift bows in a upwards curved shape under the nose as the mouth.

4. Stick one arm of your family's elf through one of the bows to stabilize him on the mirror.

Want to make it even more fun?

⭐ Instead of making a smiley face, make a Christmas tree.

⭐ Spell out a message with the bows.

⭐ Position the bows as if the mirror is a rock-climbing wall and your elf is using the bows to climb up.

WHIRLIGIG

You spin me right around baby, right around like a record player...

Here's what you'll need:

→ Ceiling fan

→ Disposable face mask

→ Toilet paper tube

→ Painting tape (or any kind of tape that won't damage your ceiling fan blades when it's removed)

Set it up:

1. Slide your elf inside the toilet paper tube so that it fits around his torso. Secure him in it with some tape.

2. Wrap the face mask around the toilet tube and secure it with tape. Just tape the mask itself around the tube – don't tape the elastic ear loops because you'll need them for the next step).

3. Gather the two ear loops of the mask together and gently stick one of the fan blades through them so that the elf is suspended from the blade. Place a little tape on top of the ear loops so that your elf will remain hanging from the blade even when the fan is turned on.

4. Do a test run by turning the fan on to make sure your elf doesn't fly out.

5. The next morning, turn the fan on just before your kids wake up.

Want to make it even more fun?

If your elf really wants to make a mess:

⭐ Attach a small, open but empty elf-sized jar to his hands and spread glitter, confetti, or sprinkles all over the floor below him.

⭐ Stage some rubber ducks and spread out some croutons on the floor. Tape a crouton bag to your elf's hand so that he "feeds" the ducks as he's swinging around.

WORST CHRISTMAS COOKIES EVER!

*How can your pets eat these cookies?!?
Something definitely went wrong
in the ratio of ingredients!*

Here's what you'll need:

➜ A bowl of dry pet food

➜ A small cup with some wet and mushed
up pieces of the dry pet food

➜ A note with the following: "Blech! These
Christmas cookies are just awful! You better not
leave these for Santa tomorrow night because
he might not leave you any presents."

Set it up:

1. Set your family's elf next to the pet food bowl, along with the cup. Lean the elf's head over a bit, as if he's spitting out the pet food into the cup.

2. Place the note nearby.

Want to make it even more fun?

⭐ Leave a roll of ready-made cookie dough (setting it out just
before your kid starts searching for the family elf) and make a
suggestion in the elf's note to "make these cookies instead."

YOU'LL NEVER GUESS WHAT THIS GIFT IS!

I've got the greatest gift all wrapped up for when you're ready to go. Can you guess what it is? Hint #1: It's very useful. Hint #2: It's great for all ages. Hint #3: It can be used while sitting or standing.

Here's what you'll need:

➔ A large roll of gift wrap

➔ A bow

➔ Lots of tape

➔ A clean toilet

Got it up:

1. Gift wrap the entire toilet and place a bow on it.

Want to make it even more fun?

⭐ Substitute the toilet paper with a small roll of gift wrap or Scotch tape.

ABOUT THE
AUTHOR

An expert in all things festive, Mr. Elf Delphine has spent years delighting his family with hilarious antics and playful surprises. As the North Pole's resident jokester, his pranks have been known to lead to unexpected trouble – especially when put in charge of keeping Santa's naughty list in check! With a flair for the comedic, Mr. Delphine's whimsical pranks have been known to land him in hot water with Santa on more than one occasion.

When he's not causing mischief at the North Pole, Mr. Delphine loves visiting families and bringing his humorous touch to their holiday traditions. Whether he's decorating the living room with a year's supply of toilet paper or just rolling around in sprinkles, he's on a mission to help everyone fully embrace the joy of the season.